# *Beyond Kankey Hill*

## A memoir by Albert J. Williams

Copyright © 2022 Albert J. Williams. All Rights Reserved. No part of this publication may be used or reproduced in any manner whatsoever without written permission from the publisher, except in the case of brief quotations embodied in critical articles and reviews.

ISBN: 9798377458685

Edited and Designed by Victor Rook (victorrook.com)

I dedicate this book to my beloved, late sister, Doris Elizabeth Williams.

# TABLE OF CONTENTS

ACKNOWLEDGMENTS ................................................. vi

A SLICE OF MY FAMILY TREE ................................ vii

PROLOGUE ................................................................. xii

CHAPTER 1: My Life Growing Up in Virginia ................ 1

CHAPTER 2: School Days ............................................. 35

CHAPTER 3: March On Washington August 28, 1963 .. 47

CHAPTER 4: The Army Life ......................................... 51

CHAPTER 5: Moving To New York .............................. 60

CHAPTER 6: Trips to Europe ........................................ 79

CHAPTER 7: Show Business ......................................... 91

CHAPTER 8: Moving Back to Virginia ....................... 113

# ACKNOWLEDGMENTS

I wish to acknowledge with much love and gratitude to a few friends and family members who provided me with important information in writing this memoir. First of all, I want to thank my cousin Rhonda Brown (daughter of my aunt Margaret Bell) for giving me loads of family information and sending me pictures of our grandmother Ora Bell and other relatives. To three of my nieces, Barbara Williams, Brenda Woodbridge, and Margaret Parham, I thank you for your input concerning how we made something out of nothing while we were growing up in Woodbridge. To my New York friends, Karla Deer, Sharolyn McCreary, and Laurell Fogle, I thank you all for the expertise you provided me with in resolving my computer woes, even when I called any of you late at night to help fix a computer technical problem. Loads of thanks go to my dear friend, Helen Smith, for sharing remembrances. Lastly, my thanks to Lynda Silverstrand for her invaluable help, patience, encouragement, and giving me my first interview on January 24, 2019. If I have failed to mention anyone else who may have contributed to these writings, the failure was not intentional.

# A SLICE OF MY FAMILY TREE

Albert Joseph Williams – born January 28, 1941.
Corinne Odella Bell – Albert's mother born June 2, 1908 – died February 24, 1943.
Charles Williams – Albert's father born May 3, 1903 – died August 7, 1971.
Charles Herbert Williams – Albert's oldest brother born July 29, 1927 – died January 26, 2009. He served in World War II and worked as a carpenter at Fort Belvoir Military Army Base.
James Edward Williams – Albert's younger brother born January 31, 1931 – died February 28, 1970. He served in the Korean War in the 1950s.
Doris Elizabeth Williams – Albert's only sister born March 3, 1929 – died July 5, 2002. She worked thirty years for Government Operations at the U.S. Army Engineer Center in Fort Belvoir, Virginia. On May 2, 1979, for her outstanding and substantial contribution to the U.S. Government, she received a personal written recognition from President Jimmy Carter.
Richard (Peter) Williams – Albert's oldest uncle born September 28, 1907 – died May, 21, 1975.
John Wesley Williams – Albert's youngest uncle born January 28, 1919 – died in 1982 (month unknown). He served in World War II. Richard, John, and Albert's father, Charles, were brothers.
John L. Bell – Albert's great-grandfather born 1849 (month unknown) – died 1898 (month unknown). In 1881, at the young age of 32, he became the first pastor

of Neabsco Baptist Church. The church was originally called New School Baptist Church and sat on grounds that were used by former slaves for worship on Sundays.

Jannie E. Bell (McCauley) – Albert's great-grandmother born January 15, 1859 – died June 18, 1911. She was the wife of John L. Bell. Out of that marriage came four children known as Nettie Bell, Eleanor Bell, William Bell, and Joseph Bell.

Ora Bell – Albert's grandmother born February 24, 1887, in Ireland and came to Pennsylvania (year unknown) as an indentured servant. She first married a Mr. Mills (first name unknown). They had three children: Leon, Raymond, and Morris. After Mr. Mills' death, Ora moved to Woodbridge, met Joseph Bell, and they got married. Out of that marriage came six (6) children: Corinne Bell, Frances Bell, Kathryn Bell, Margaret Bell, Alberta Bell, and Fannie Jo Bell. Margaret was very light skinned and passed as White while working at Garfinckel's Department Store in the 1950s. The store was located on 14th Street, N.W. Washington, DC, and catered to high society and wealthy White folks. Whenever my aunt Margaret, who was living in Washington at the time, visited us here in Woodbridge, she'd be dressed to the tee. Meaning, she looked fabulous. Absolutely stunning! During one of her visits, I remember seeing her dressed like a cowgirl straight from the old western movies. She was wearing a cowgirl's outfit, including the hat, boots, and ballooned trousers. She looked like Alexis Colby, played by actress Joan Collins on the TV series *Dynasty*. Ora Bell had a hobby of collecting elegantly dressed porcelain dolls. I remember seeing anywhere from 8 to 10 dolls, and all of them were White, with the exception of one that was Colored. Ora Bell died March 19th, 1955, in Prince William County, Virginia, and is buried at the Lincoln Memorial Cemetery, Suitland, Maryland, alongside her daughter, Kathryn Bell Robinson.

Joseph Bell – Albert's grandfather born October 20, 1878 – died August 6, 1918. After Joseph Bell died, Ora Bell met and married a Mr. Johnson, (first name unknown, but believed to have been James). Out of the marriage came a son named Clarence P. Johnson, whom we all called "Snookie."

Left to right: Uncle Raymond and Grandma Ora Bell seated. Women standing left to right: Aunt Margaret and Aunt Kathyrn.

My mother born Corinne Odella Bell.

My mother Corinne Williams and her brother-in-law Rob Corbin.

Aunt Margaret, who could pass as White.

# PROLOGUE

I, Albert Joseph Williams, am one of four siblings of Charles and Corinne (Bell) Williams. I got my first spanking from the doctor who delivered me from my mother's womb. Not only did he deliver and spank me, but he gave me the name Albert Joseph. The doctor's name was Alfred Joseph Ferlazzo. He was a short little Italian man who was admired, trusted, and respected by all the Colored people in Woodbridge. As I got older, I remember seeing him carrying a little black medical bag as he made individual house calls. When he opened his office in Triangle, Virginia, I would often take my father there for medical treatments.

I grew up on Bethel/Smoketown/Neabsco Mills Road in Woodbridge, Virginia. It's not that I lived on three different roads, but because Prince William County changed the name of the roads a few times. According to land records at the Prince William County Court House in Manassas, Virginia, my family's land goes back to the early 1900s. Frankly speaking, I believe it goes back to the 1800s. The reason I say that is because my great-grandfather, John Bell, at the age of 32, became the first pastor of my family's church in 1881.

In the 1950s, my great-uncle John R. Tuell deeded nine (9) acres of land to my father, Charles Williams, who divided and gave various portions of that nine acres to different family members, including me. It was believed that Mr. Tuell originally owned 30 acres. My great-aunt Jannie Johnson Dorsey owned 10 acres on the eastern side of Neabsco Mills Road. In the early 1960s, she sold those 10 acres to a doctor named Dr. Vaslequez, whom I heard was eventually deported for some unknown reason. The property is where Freedom High School sits today. Also, during the 1960s and even before that, many Colored families, (we were called Colored then) lived on this road now known as Neabsco Mills Road. In addition to the Williams family, there were the Davis family, the Kendall family, the Bowles family, the Smith family, the Thomas family and a few other Colored families. Even though some of us Coloreds were not related, we all treated each other like family. This part of Woodbridge was our own little *Peyton Place*. To my understanding, the land surrounding my family's property was part of something called Light Horse Harry Lee's Plantation, known as Leesylvania back in the 1700-1800s. The land that was once owned by my family now sits next to Northern Virginia Community College, Woodbridge Campus, and hosts the Hilton hotels and apartment buildings on Smoke Court. Presently, my house is the last piece of personal residential property on this road.

As I was growing up here in Woodbridge, I went to segregated schools and studied from used textbooks, which came from White schools. Many days on my way to school, walking in the rain and snow, I had holes in my shoes. Because my family didn't have electricity, I read and studied my homework by the light coming from an old kerosene-burning lamp. I was given used clothes from other families, mainly from a White family called the Tyrrells. With the Jim Crow laws being in effect, Colored children weren't allowed to go to school with the Whites. We Coloreds had to travel long distance to get to our school. On the way to school, we were often harassed by a few White kids. Yes, they called us the N word, made ugly faces towards us, and spit at us.

After I finished high school, I moved to Washington, DC, and attended Howard University full time during the day, and worked full time as a janitor at night with the FHA (Federal Housing Administration). In November of 1963, I started my military service with the United States Army. After serving my country, I moved to New York and worked for the Federal Reserve Bank of New York. During my tenure in New York, I became a member of the union called SAG/AFTRA (short for Screen Actors Guild/American Federation of Television Radio Artists). I worked and appeared in over 80 movies and television shows with some of the world's most famous people in show business. New York was very good to me.

But in 2001, my sister became very ill, and I was traveling back and forth from New York to Woodbridge a few times each month. After she died on July 5, 2002, which was one of the saddest days of my life, I moved back to Woodbridge. It wasn't as segregated as it was when I left in January of 1966. It was a little more diverse. But I must say, during my youth when I was growing up here in Woodbridge, there was a lot of segregation. Movie houses and theatre outlets had specific bathrooms. One for "Whites Only" and one for "Coloreds." There weren't that many places to go shopping. The community didn't have much industry or opportunities for "Colored" folks. However, the county started to change in the early 1960s with the creation of Interstate 95 and Dale City. Also, the Marumsco Plaza, which was not too friendly to people of color, was built in the 1960s. Years later, in the 1980s, Potomac Mills Shopping Center was built.

# CHAPTER 1
# My Life Growing Up in Virginia

One of my favorite writers, Ms. Harper Lee, wrote one book that impacted my whole life. That book was called *To Kill a Mocking Bird*. Well, I'm no Harper Lee, and this might be my only book, but I hope it helps someone. By the way, this year, 2010, the year I started writing this memoir, is the 50$^{th}$ anniversary of the book by Ms. Harper Lee.

I remember one time in the late 1940s, my sister, whose real name is Doris (but we all called her Sis), dressing me up in a little kid's Navy military outfit. She put a little white Navy cap on my head and had me put on a blue shirt and blue bell-bottom pants. I believe my brother Charles Jr., whom we all called "Puddin," brought the outfit for me because we had an uncle, John Wesley Williams, serving in the Navy at the time. By my sister putting that outfit on me, it made me look like a little kid in the Navy.

When our mom died on February 24, 1943, I was only 2 years and 11 months old. My sister was 14, and she became my mom. Because we both were very young, I don't remember our maternal mother. Not only was Sis young, but she was attractive and very vulnerable at age 14. After our mother died and our father had gone to work, strange old men started hanging around our house. As Sis and I became much older, she told me that when she was very young she was forced sexually (raped) by an older man. Out of that horrible experience, at the young tender age of 14, she got pregnant. A year or so later, with consent, she became pregnant twice by a different man. Eight or nine years later, still with consent, she became pregnant by a third man. Although Sis never married, similar things were happening to other young Colored girls in our neighborhood.

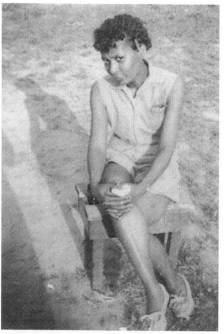

My sister Doris Williams.

Sis was a good mother, and she would often tell me how glad she was that I helped her raise her children. Sis and I were *children* raising *children*. I couldn't have had a better mother than Sis. Some of her children were pretty close to my age. Because I was a little bit older than them, I felt I should be telling them what to do. They didn't like that, and as I got older, I realize why. I guess they felt that, because they were close to my age, I had no business telling them what to do. In reality, I only wanted the best for them. I loved those kids. I cared about them. I wanted them to go to school and be educated.

I remember when my sister's children and I got home from school, I was the one that prepared the meals for them. I wanted the children to be properly nourished by making sure they ate their meals, even though most of the meals were hot dogs and pork and beans. In addition, I wanted them to learn how to be responsible. So, each day after school, I assigned different chores to each of them. Chores such as bringing in logs of wood, kindlin' wood, washing dishes, getting the laundry ready for washing, etc. I did these things so that when Sis got home from work, she wouldn't have so much to do.

Before she started working at Fort Belvoir, Virginia, Sis had worked a few other jobs when she was young. As a teenager, she carried me in her arms as she worked at a diner called Porter's Inn, located in Dumfries, Virginia. Sis also worked at a restaurant called Steve's Inn in Woodbridge, Virginia.

Even though this was the 1950s, our family didn't have running water. We got our water from a nearby spring down in the woods. That spring was right behind what's now called Northern Virginia Community College, and the spring ran all the way down into Neabsco Creek at Route One (Jefferson Davis Highway). Our house sat on a hill west of Bethel Road (now called Neabsco Mills Road). At the time, I had a little red wagon. In that wagon, Sis and I would put an old galvanized tub, a washboard, some Octagon soap, dirty clothes, and anything else that would fit into that wagon. Then we would head down to the spring, dirty clothes and all. Once we got to the spring, we'd take some water from it, put that water in the galvanized tub, and wash the dirty clothes right there at the spring. Once the clothes were all washed, Sis and I took them back home and hung them on the outdoor homemade clothesline. Sometimes, we hung the clothes on tree branches. I remember there were a lot of diapers with yellow stains. Pampers weren't around then.

Most of the Coloreds that lived in this part of Woodbridge were catching hell. We were poor but not desperate. We lived just above Kankey Hill, which was a steep hill that started at the southern part of Bethel Road at the intersection of Jefferson Davis Highway. Today, there is a huge church known as the Harvest Life Ministries on that hill. It was said that the hill was called Kankey Hill because right above it lived a cluster of Colored people with kinkey, kankey hair. That cluster of Colored people extended about half a mile north on Bethel Road.

Years later, the name of the road was changed from Bethel Road to Smoketown Road. All the Colored people lived on the left and north side of Bethel Road, just above Kankey Hill. Friends and family members had told me that the name of the road was changed to Smoketown Road because there were a lot of "smoky, dark-looking people" living on that road.

Kankey Hill was always full of trees and wildlife. It was the hill where I sat many times waiting for my sister to return with food from Doc Hampton's Log Cabin Store or from Laura Kincheloe's Country Store. Our daddy, Shack, had an account at both stores, and Sis would often go there to get food on that account. I would just sit there amongst the trees on Kankey Hill and wait for Sis. Sometimes it seemed like I waited for hours, just sitting there on the ground, on a log, or on a rock. At times, I would see rabbits, squirrels, or deer moving about, and I'd wonder if my sister was going to be able to get us some food to eat. There were a few times my sister would come back empty-handed. Even though that didn't happen too often, it happened. Mainly, it happened when my father's credit bill wasn't paid up to date. If Sis wasn't able to get any food at the stores, she would sadly return to the woods of Kankey Hill and see me sitting and waiting there for her. We would go back home, get a pail or some kind of container, and we would walk up and down Bethel Road and pick huckleberries or blackberries. Some of the old blackberry bushes are still there today. If we had any bread or flour, we would put it into the mixture of those berries to make the meal thicker and larger. We called that mixture Blackberry Mush. I've eaten many dishes of it.

Today's blackberries don't taste like the wild ones Sis and I picked in the 1950s. The berries today are very hard to digest. But they sure were mighty good when I was growing up. When our father's credit was in good standing at either one of the two country stores, Sis would come back with things such as bread, bologna, Spam, dry beans, hot dogs, cans of pork and beans, and mayonnaise. I remember eating many mayonnaise sandwiches.

Besides not having running water, we didn't have electricity either. As previously stated, we got most of our water from the nearby spring. However, when some of our neighbors did get a well, we would get water from them. Across the street from us there lived a White family called the Tripletts. They had running water and let us get water from them. Most of us Coloreds had wood-burning stoves. Sometimes when my daddy Shack had a few extra dollars, he would go and get wood from Mr. Simmons, who was a White man that lived near Davis Ford Road, now called Minnieville Road. Mr. Simmons was in the business of sawing, selling, and delivering wood to anyone who could afford to pay. I remember one time me and my father went to Mr. Simmons and ordered a truckload of wood (we called it a cord of wood at that time). Mr. Simmons said, "Y'all live down there by Kankey Hill?" My father told him that we did. If Mr. Simmons told you he was going to bring the wood at a certain time, like 4 p.m. or 5 p.m., believe me, he would be on time, to get that money.

My family used the wood for cooking on the stove in the kitchen and in the old wore-out stove we had in the living room. There were times when it was so cold in the house and no one had any money, we would just cook on the old stove in the living room.

Old stove in my father's house.

Our house was not in the best condition. It seemed like it was always cold inside during the winter. Window panes were either missing or broken. Sis and I would put a blanket or anything we could get our hands on to block out the cold air coming in through the missing panes. If Sis did any ironing in the evenings, after she got finished she'd wrap that warm iron up in a towel and put it at the bottom of my bed to keep my feet warm. My feet stayed cold a lot. We made the best of what we had, and believe me, life was no bowl of cherries. My father, my brothers, and people from the neighborhood would spend hours in the woods chopping down trees and sawing wood. We would give everyone some of the wood because, like I said, most of us Coloreds had wood-burning stoves.

Iron Sis would use to iron clothes and keep my feet warm.

Around the holidays, like Thanksgiving and Christmas, Sis tried to fix up the house a little bit. She would get a few rolls of wallpaper and make a paste out of white flour. She'd mix that paste with a small amount of water and slap it on the backside of the wallpaper. Then she took one end of the wallpaper, got on a chair, and hung it. I stayed on the floor and held the other end. The house was beginning to look livable. To get a Christmas tree, I would go down in the woods near Uncle John Wesley's house and cut down a tree. Sis decorated the tree with all kinds of hand-me-down ornaments, which mostly came from the Tyrrells.

A year or so later, our father Shack dug a well 62 feet deep. My two brothers, Puddin and Jimmy, would bucket our father down into the big deep hole. Once down in the hole, Shack would dig and dig. He would fill the bucket up with dirt, and my two brothers would pull it up from the hole. When the hole was less than 62 feet deep, Shack would tie about six sticks of dynamite on a rope, light that dynamite, and drop it down into the hole. When the dynamite exploded, it made the hole deeper and wider. Later on, Shack would gather buckets of gravel and go back down in that hole. He would put layers and layers of gravel in the hole. I was told that the gravel was used to make the water crystal clear.

I remember one day Shack asked me if I wanted to get in the bucket with him and go down in the hole. I said, "Sure." So, I got in the bucket, which was big enough for both of us. Puddin and Jimmy proceeded to let me and Shack down into the well. When we got down to the bottom, I saw rocks, sand, and crystal-clear water. As I looked upwards to the sky, the hole appeared very, very small. I could hardly wait till I got back up and out of that well. It was a frightening experience. I said to myself that I would never ever go in that well hole again. I loved my father, but that experience was a little too much for me. Though I must say, that was some good-drinking well water. Today, when I think of going down in that well hole, I can imagine how Joseph felt when his brothers threw him in the well during the biblical days.

My brother Charles Jr. ("Puddin") Williams.

My brother James Williams.

## ALBERT J. WILLIAMS

Like his brother John Wesley, Shack owned a few chickens and pigs too. In order to get feed for the pigs, Shack would walk from his house on Bethel Road all the way over to what's now known as Cardinal Drive and Minnieville Road. It was at least a six-mile walk each way. There was a little country store right off Minnieville Road where my father would go and buy a 50-lb bag of feed for the hogs. He would then make that long journey back home with that 50-lb bag on his shoulders.

When the month of November came around, it was time to slaughter pigs. The whole process was disgusting to me. First, Shack would take a shotgun and shoot the pig in the head. The next step was to put the dead pig in a big 500-gallon barrel of boiling hot water heated on a pile of burning logs. After about thirty minutes or longer, Shack, along with other men from the neighborhood, would take the pig out of the barrel and hang it up on a tall wooden scaffold. They then took a knife, scraped all the hair off the pig, and cut the pig wide open. Because the sight of so much blood was making me sick, I temporarily closed my eyes. The next thing I saw was the pig being cut up into various pieces. Some pieces of meat were given to the neighbors who helped Shack with the pig. Nearly every part of that pig would eventually be eaten, from the feet to the tail. Even the intestines, known as chitterlings, would be eaten.

Another thing I remembered my dad doing was fishing. Whenever he wasn't working and I didn't have school, we would go fishing. Shack would wake me up in the morning around 4 a.m. and tell me, "We're gonna go fishing." Sleepily, I would get up, wash, and get dressed. Shack would gather an old bucket and the homemade fish net, which he had made out of chicken net wire. The net hung at the end of a wooden pole, which extended outward about 12 feet. This wooden pole was now a homemade fishing pole. Next, he'd get the old kerosene-burning lantern and give it to me. Off we went down Bethel Road, cross Jefferson Davis Highway, and fish in Neabsco Creek, which was located right off Jefferson Davis Highway and Blackburn Road.

The early mornings would be so dark. Once we got to the creek, I held the lantern so Shack could see the fish. The water was very clear and one could see schools of fish. Shack would dip up a whole school of fish, put them in the bucket, and we'd head back home. I liked fishing but didn't like getting up so early in the mornings. When we got home, we would clean the fish, put them in mason jars, add salt, and seal the jars. Now we would have food, pork and salted fish, for the winter. It was a time when many people, especially the Coloreds, didn't give much thought about salt and high blood pressure. That's probably why so many of us suffered with it. Certainly, salted fish and too much pork were contributing factors.

Where I would fish with my dad on Neabsco Creek.

Besides fishing and slaughtering pigs, Shack did little odd jobs around the county. For example, he worked for a while at the power plant on Possum Point in Dumfries, Virginia. He would get up in the mornings, wash, get dressed, put on an old baseball cap, walk down Bethel Road to Jefferson Davis Highway, turn right, and walk south to Possum Point. He walked to and from that job almost every day. There were times when someone would see him walking and give him a ride. Almost everyone, Blacks and Whites, in the areas of Woodbridge, Triangle, and Dumfries knew Shack.

There was a time when he worked for a White family called the Hamptons. Mr. Hampton, whom everyone called "Doc Hampton," and his family, lived right at Leesylvania Park by a marina they owned in Woodbridge, Virginia. Doc's wife's name was Goldie, and they had two girls and one boy. Shack dug a well for them. During the summer, I would do their yard work, such as trimming shrubberies and cutting the grass with Shack's old-fashioned grass cutter, which he called a "Grass Scissile."

One of the grass sickles my father used to use.

## BEYOND KANKEY HILL

On the same side of the street where the Hampton's house was located, there was a big swimming pool. I believe the pool was owned or leased by the same people that owned the Pilot House Restaurant, which was a big ship that sat in the waters of the Potomac River right across the street from the Hamptons. The Pilot House Restaurant was only a stone's throw from dry land. My job was to clean up the trash and cigarette butts around the pool. Keep the area clean. Gambling took place on the ship. But because I was underage (and Colored), I wasn't allowed to go on the ship. The whole surrounding area was known as "Freestone Point." I don't remember ever seeing Colored people in the area. All the Whites seemed to be upper bourgeois and very affluent while congregating on the ship and around the pool. The whole scene sort of reminded me of the Monte-Carlo resort on the French Riviera. If one ever visits Leesylvania Park, there's a picture of how that area looked back in the 1950s and early 1960s.

Before I could work there, I had to get a work permit from the courthouse in Manassas, Virginia. I believe I was 15 or 16 years old. I didn't mind working. The extra money would help me buy my books and get clothes for school. I could even help my sister get something for her children. For me, helping my sister with the children was quite a task. Like I said before, my sister and I were *children* taking care of *children*. I remember she and I, along with other kids from the neighborhood, would often wait for the Good Humor Ice Cream truck to come by our house. We'd listen for the bell or chimes and gather our coins. There were times when my sister would ask the Good Humor Man if he had any extra blocks of ice. If he did, he would give us a block. My sister would take that block of ice and wrap it up in newspaper. She did that in order to keep it from melting so fast. We had an old portable icebox, and that's where my sister would put the newspaper-wrapped ice and hoped that it would not melt so fast. If we wanted ice for our drinks, we would take an old ice pick, remove some of the newspaper from the block of ice, and chop off pieces for our drinks. We made a lot of lemonade and drank a lot of Kool-Aid back then in the 1950s. When the block of ice melted and we didn't have any left, we would take our favorite bottled drinks, like Nehi, Root Beer, and Coke Cola, down to the spring in the woods in the back of our house. We'd put the bottled drinks in that spring of cold running water so they would keep cold. So, whenever we wanted a cold drink, we would go to the spring to get one.

That spring came in handy many times. I remember there were times when Sis cooked a pot of beans and we'd have some left over. Because we didn't have a refrigerator, we would take that pot of leftover beans down to that old spring. Once there at the spring, we would sit the pot of beans down in the spring of water. That way, the beans would not spoil. Another thing we ate quite a bit of was something called Poke Salad. It was a wide, leafy green vegetable one could find growing on the roadside or in the woods. You picked it, washed it, and cooked it just like you would kale, mustard greens, or collards. Yes, times were hard in the 1950s, but no matter what, we always had something to eat. Even if it was nothing but berries, such as blackberries, strawberries, elderberries, or huckleberries.

Sis and I, along with others in the neighborhood, would often pick some of those wild berries on the roadside of Bethel Road. Some of the berries we would give to my uncle John Wesley. He had served in the Navy during World War II, and he made the best homemade berry wines anywhere. His house was just down the hill near the creek in the back of our house. Today, the Homewood Suites owned by Hilton Hotels sits on that spot where Uncle John's house once stood. The old house had upstairs that were very steep. It was the same house originally owned by my great-great-aunt Jane E. Williams, who was born in the late 1880s.

My great-great-uncle John R. Tuell lived next door to Aunt Jane. I don't know much about Uncle Tuell, other than as a child I remember seeing him with his hands behind his back walking around the property. I also remember he had an old meat house where he hung smoked meats like hams, turkeys, ducks, and chickens from the ceiling. I read somewhere that he once owned 30 acres of land. There are records in the Manassas courthouse showing where Uncle Tuell deeded nine acres to my father, Charles Williams, Sr. After Jane and Tuell died, my great-aunt Irene (one of three daughters of Jane), took over the house. I had been told by other family members that my great-great-aunt Jane E. Williams, who was in a wheelchair, fell down the stairs from the top floor of her old house and eventually died from her injuries.

When I was 10 or 11 years old, I remember Aunt Irene making homemade butter. I can see her now, pushing and pulling up and down an old wooden churn. She would churn the milk until it turned into butter. The cakes Aunt Irene made from that homemade butter were so good. Even the cornbread she made tasted like cake. Besides being a good cook, Aunt Irene was a good domestic person. She washed, starched, and iron clothes to make them look new. She used an old heavy-duty cast iron to iron clothes.

There was a White family that lived near Telegraph Road in Woodbridge. The area was often called "Agnesville." Every few weeks, an old Colored man everyone called Mr. Lucas, who stood about 5' 5", would gather dirty clothes from that White family. He'd pack those dirty clothes in an old beat-up suitcase and bring them to Aunt Irene so she could wash, starch, and iron them. Although Mr. Lucas lived right on Telegraph Road, it was quite a distance for him to walk. It must had been at least five miles going and five miles coming. Three or four days later, he would return and pick up the nicely washed, starched, and pressed clean clothes from Aunt Irene. Then he'd make that long walk back to the White folks and drop off the clothes.

After Aunt Irene died, my uncle John Wesley stayed in the house. The house didn't have running water, but there was a small well about 15 or 20 feet deep in the back yard. Because there was no running water in the house, John Wesley made an outdoor homemade shower. He took an old empty 50-gallon barrel, cut out the entire top, and cut a 2-inch hole in the bottom of the barrel. The piece he cut from the bottom he attached a long string to it and used that piece as a water shower stopper plug. He would climb up the ladder and put the 50-gallon barrel on top of the scaffolds that he had made. The scaffolds extended about 12 feet vertically. After connecting the 50-gallon barrel to the top of the scaffolds, he'd come down off that ladder and start making many trips with buckets of water up and down that ladder. He got the water from the small well that was in the back yard. Once the barrel was filled with water, he would wait a few days so the sun could heat the water. Finally, he had a homemade shower. When he pulled the string, warm or hot water came out.

John Wesley was always very creative. In the back yard of his house, he made a fish pond. He put small gold fish in that pond, but it seemed like every few weeks he was putting new ones in because they kept dying. Finally, he got fed up and turned that fish pond into a flower garden. One could see the garden from the back porch of the house.

That old house had a few rooms upstairs and a few rooms downstairs. One of the rooms downstairs he turned into a bar room. It even had four or five barstools and a string of red, blue, and green lights that hung from the ceiling. Although the space was very small, it was very cozy. John Wesley even had an old record player. On that record player, he would play his old and new 78 rpm or 45 rpm records. Every now and then, he had to put a new needle in the arm so the records wouldn't skip. Because he liked music, seemed like every week he was buying a new record. Some of his favorite artists were Fats Domino, Lloyd Price, Etta James, Ruth Brown, LaVern Baker, Ray Charles, Johnny Cash, Brenda Lee, and Patsy Cline.

In addition to liking music, John Wesley liked his Kentucky bourbon whiskey and his homemade wine. There were times when he even made wine from wild dandelions, raisins, peaches, and potatoes. Nearly everyone on Bethel Road, and in Woodbridge for that matter, loved John Wesley's homemade wine. The wine he made tasted just as good, if not better than the wines sold in stores today. I remember two sisters from the Chinn's family would often visit John Wesley. When those two sisters came from John Wesley's house, they were high as a kite. Older people would say, "they were tipsy."

# ALBERT J. WILLIAMS

Uncle John Wesley and Sis in 1967.

Almost everyone admired John Wesley. He raised chickens. Every year he would order a box full of baby chicks from some farming magazine. Once those chicks were grown, they started to lay eggs. John Wesley would give most of those eggs to people in the neighborhood or to people he worked for. He was just a kind and giving person who believed in sharing. A few times he asked me to clean out the chicken coop, which I dreaded. One time I got a buddy of mine to help me. Let me tell you what we did. We got some Easter egg dye and dyed some of those baby chicks. We dyed them red, blue, or whatever color we came up with. John Wesley came out of the house cursing and swearing. He told us to go home and don't come back. He was mad as you can be. I tell you one thing, he never asked me to clean out that chicken coop again. Now days, the more I think of it, what my buddy and I did to those poor little chicks was a cruel thing. Horrible. Then again, we weren't the only ones doing bad things to animals back then.

I remember one of my sister's boyfriends putting some kittens in an old feed sack that looked like a big pillowcase. Once he had put all the kittens in the sack, he tied up the sack so the kittens couldn't get out. Then he got in his car and I rode with him. I had no idea where he was going. Next thing I knew, we were at a creek right off of Spriggs Road near Minnieville Road. He put that sack of poor little kittens in the creek to drown. I was shocked. I hated seeing him do that. I thought it was terrible. I thought he would have let the kittens out on the roadside or somewhere.

Another thing I witnessed when I was young was an elderly lady doing harm to a cat. She befriended the cat, tied a piece of string with empty beer cans on it, and attached the string to the tail of the cat. Then she poured turpentine on the cat's tail. The cat screamed, hollered, and ran like a bat out of hell. So, you see, what my friend and I did to John Wesley's baby chicks wasn't as bad as what other people did to animals.

Other than chickens, John Wesley owned a cow, a horse, pigs, and even a goat. Most of those critters scared me. The cow would chase me. The red rooster would chase me. The goat would chase me. Of all those animals, I think the goat was the worst. John Wesley kept that horrible, stinking thing tied up most of the time. Somehow at night, it would break loose and end up on the porch of the house where me and my father lived. I don't know what it was, but those animals just didn't like me, and I sure didn't like them.

## ALBERT J. WILLIAMS

John Wesley was a very good cook. In fact, he worked as the main cook at a restaurant in Fort Belvoir. The restaurant, called Ruby's Restaurant, was located on the left side of Route 1 going north just above Accotink Creek. It was owned and operated by Mr. and Mrs. Tate, who were White, and allowed only Whites inside. On the front of the building was a big sign over the entrance door that read, "Whites Only." One summer John Wesley got me a job at the restaurant working as a dishwasher. I didn't mind washing those dirty dishes and pans. At least I had a job for the summer. Around 4 a.m. or 5 a.m., he would stop by my house and we would walk down Bethel Road to Route 1 to catch the Greyhound bus going north on Route 1. The Greyhound bus stop was right in front of Doc Hampton's Log Cabin Country Store. (Today, there's a 7-Eleven store in that spot). Once we boarded the Greyhound bus, we would arrive at the restaurant about 30 or 40 minutes later, depending on the traffic. He had a key to the restaurant. However, we were not allowed to come through the front door. We had to enter through the back door.

The restaurant catered mostly to the soldiers of Fort Belvoir and the surrounding neighbors in the area. I would often peek out to the dining area and all I could see were White folks. On some weekends, Mr. and Mrs. Tate would visit John Wesley at his home here in Woodbridge. They'd drive down the old dirt road, which was right behind my father's (Charles Williams, Sr.) house. That old dirt road led right up to John Wesley's house. I tell you, when Mr. and Mrs. Tate came out from John Wesley's house, they would be, yes, mighty "tipsy." I guess they drank some of his homemade wine. I know one thing, Mrs. Tate cursed like a sailor. When I was working at the restaurant, I heard

Mrs. Tate curse Mr. Tate out so many times. She would use every curse word one could think of. But I never heard him curse back at her. John Wesley told me that it was the same way when they came down to visit him. They were a piece of work. But they never said anything nasty to me or him.

On some weekends, when he didn't have to work at the restaurant, John Wesley would do yard work for a White lady named Mrs. Redman, who was a widow and lived in Alexandria. Her house was situated not far from a lake where a lot of ducks always hung around. To make the journey to Alexandria, John Wesley would board the old Greyhound bus or hitchhike if the bus was late. He did little things around the house for her such as light painting, washing windows, trimming rose bushes, and cutting the grass. He often took me to work with him, I guess because he knew I needed money for the upcoming school year. It seemed like Mrs. Redman was just a little old lady who needed someone to talk with sometimes. The reason I say that is because when John Wesley and I would arrive at her house, she would summon us to come on into the kitchen. Once we were in the kitchen, Mrs. Redman, who was always very pleasant, would offer us sandwiches, like tuna fish, and bologna and cheese. She had all kinds of snacks for us to nibble on. Then she would start telling us stories of her family and her life. She'd go on and on and on. After listening to her for nearly 30 minutes or more, I would excuse myself and go work in the yard. After all, I came there to work.

I would go outside and cut a little bit of grass, although there wasn't much grass to cut. After I finished cutting the grass, I went down to the lake and watched the ducks. Some days, I was so bored when she kept John Wesley cooped up in that house and the two of them chatting away. Him and her would talk for hours. I was ready to go home. I remember one time in the month of August. It was so hot. Temperature must have been over a hundred degrees. Mrs. Redman peeked her head out the door and said, "Albert, come on in here. It's hot out there." I obliged and trotted to the house. There I would find John Wesley with a cup in his hands, sitting at the kitchen table. I believe that cup contained more than just coffee or tea. Mrs. Redman turns to me and says, "You want a soda pop?" I'd say, "yes, ma'm." The two of them reminded me of Miss Daisy and Hoke in the movie *Driving Miss Daisy*.

Mrs. Redman always treated me and John Wesley with respect. After leaving Mrs. Redman's house, he and I would take the Greyhound bus back to Woodbridge. But not before he stopped at a liquor store in Alexandria to pick up his bottle of Kentucky bourbon. After that, we'd catch the Greyhound bus going south to Richmond and get off at the bus stop located across from Doc Hampton's Log Cabin Country store. Then we headed up Kankey Hill to get home. I would go to my house, and John Wesley, before he went home, he'd stop and visit some of the Colored neighbors in the area.

He always carried a shopping bag with him. Lots of times when he went to work, he'd have eggs in that shopping bag and gave them to his employer. Then when he returned from work, he'd have that same shopping bag. But this time the bag would contain no eggs; it would have stuff that his employer had given him. Not only that, but somewhere in that shopping bag would be a bottle of Kentucky bourbon. He would share that bourbon with the neighbors and then go on home. John Wesley believed in giving and sharing.

He wasn't a selfish man and believed in going to church. He was a deacon at our family church, Neabsco Baptist Church in Woodbridge. It was the same church where my great-aunt Irene and my mother, Corinne, had been the church's clerks in the 1930s and 1940s. My great-grandfather, Rev. John Bell, at the age of 34, was the first minister of that church in 1881. When I was around 17 or 18 years old, I taught Sunday school at the church. I liked going to church back then and even like going now. I've been going to church all my life. I know it's my faith that sustains me and keeps me going, even to this day. For I still believe "faith is the substance of things hoped for and the evidence of things not seen." I can't see myself ever losing my faith in God. For He is the soul of my existence. Without Him, I'm nothing.

As for Uncle John Wesley, I believe he felt the same way. There were times I heard him talking to himself. Everyone in the neighborhood knew John Wesley talked to himself. I could never make out what he was saying. But I truly believe he was talking to the Lord.

Uncle John Wesley, who was light skinned, jet-black hair, and looked mulatto, took sick in 1982. He went to the local hospital called Potomac Hospital located here in Woodbridge. It was there that he was diagnosed with cancer. The last time I went to the hospital to see him, he was unconscious. He was lying on his side and was pale as a ghost. A lot of his hair was lying right there on the pillow. The loss of hair was caused by the cancer treatment. He passed away in August of 1982. Respectfully, his funeral was held at our family's church, Neabsco Baptist Church on Cardinal Drive in Woodbridge.

In the 1940s, the church didn't have a pool to baptize its members. But a little way up the road from the church was a swimming hole way back in the woods. The swimming hole was known as "Baptizing Hole" and ran all the way down to Neabsco Creek near Route 1 and Blackburn Road. That creek flows out to the Potomac River. When I was a young teenager in the 1950s, I used to go swimming in that "Baptizing Hole." It was a good place for us Colored kids to go swimming. I remember one time as I was swimming, I turned around and all of a sudden I saw a snake coming straight towards me. I believe it was a water moccasin snake. I got out of that waterhole as fast as I could. That snake scared the daylight out of me. I never went back to that hole again.

Family and friends told me that, because of the proximity of "Baptizing Hole" to the family church, the hole was used for baptizing slaves and members of our church. You see, before the church was built, the spot was used for slaves to worship on Sunday mornings. That spot was known as "Brush Harbor" or "Brush Church." After the Civil War ended and the Reconstruction Era began, slaves and former slaves decided to build a structured church. On December 5, 1881, the deed to the church was signed by my great-grandfather, Rev. John Bell, and others. The church was originally called New School Baptist Church before it became Neabsco Baptist Church. Most of my family is buried in the cemetery in the back of the church. Every Memorial Day, I put flowers on my family's graves.

I was brought up in that church. My favorite church time of each year was always the second Sunday in August. It was known as "Homecoming." It was a time when most of the old timers who had moved away would return to the church. People would be laughing and greeting others whom they hadn't seen in a long time. Two church services were done on that second Sunday in August. One service was done in the a.m. and the other in the p.m. Between 1 p.m. and 3 p.m., dinner was served. Food would be everywhere on the tables, which had been placed outside next to the church. You see, everyone dined outside because the church didn't have an inside dining room. Some people sat inside their cars. Others would sit on the ground. Some of the foods were homemade cornbread, corn pudding, collard greens, ham, bread pudding, and homemade cakes and pies. Yes, there was fried chicken too. It was the best fried chicken north of Louisiana. You talk about good food? That was some good eating!

A little before 3 p.m., after everyone had their bellies full, the people would gather back inside the church and wait for the guest preacher to start preaching. Sometimes, a guest preacher would be so boring that people would start falling asleep. Even I almost fell asleep, until I got a punch from someone sitting next to me. Then again, there were times when the church would engage a fiery guest preacher. One that would have the church people going crazy and certainly kept you from falling asleep. I remember people hollering, shouting, passing out, screaming, and running down the aisles. To me, those people really had the Holy Ghost. They were God-fearing people and praising God. But the way they were carrying on, I was surprised that some of that food they had just eaten didn't come back up. Yes, we Colored people, as we were called back then, enjoyed "Home Coming" in August.

Another thing I enjoyed during my early youth was that of grapevine swinging. You see, me and some of the other kids in the neighborhood would often go in the woods and swing on the old grapevines. The vines were old, strong, and hung from huge trees. We pretended to be like Tarzan and swung on those old grapevines. We even made that "holler" like Tarzan did in the old television series. We would swing and swing. Lucky we didn't kill ourselves. A few times we fell, but nothing serious. We had fun.

On most weekends, because my family and I didn't have a TV, I would go over to my neighbor's house and watch their TV. I watched shows such as *The Lone Ranger*, *The Little Rascals*, *Abbott and Costello*, *Randolph Scott*, *Lassie*, *Leave It To Beaver*, *Father Knows Best*, *Hit Parade*, *The Loretta Young Show*, *The Lawrence Welk Show*, *The Perry Como Show*, *The Nat King Cole Show*, and *The Ed Sullivan Show*. I enjoyed all those shows. They were very entertaining.

I was still a young teenager, maybe 15 or 16, when the foregoing happened. As I got a bit older, my father and I built a little house for me in the back of our big house. Now I had my *own* house. I was proud of that little house. It was made of old leftover plywood, lumber, tarpaper, and scrap pieces that my father had found somewhere along the way. My father was good at building things. Him and I built my little house in about thirty days. For cooking, someone gave me an old gas stove that used propane gas. I brought the propane tank and put it on the outside of my newfound home. I was very excited.

When I had saved up enough money, I went out and brought myself a black and white TV. Well, let me tell you this. I think it will make you laugh. I went to a hardware store located in Occoquan, Virginia. There I purchased a piece of plexiglass. I guess it was about 24 inches. It had three colors. It was blue at the top, red in the middle, and green at the bottom. When I got home, I cut that plexiglass down to the size of my TV screen, which I believe was 21 inches. I then taped the multicolored plexiglass over my black and white TV. Viola! I now had a color TV! The blue at the top was the sky, the red in the middle was the people, and that green at the bottom was the grass. When people visited me in my little house, they were very impressed. To tell you the truth, I was too. All of that happened right after the invention of color TV in 1953.

That little house helped me out quite a bit. You see, during that time I was still in high school. I needed money to buy school supplies and clothes. I am not proud of this, but I became a bootlegger. I would give an adult money to buy me half a gallon of liquor. I would then pour that liquor into half-pint bottles and sell them to customers. Sometimes, customers would be knocking on my door as early as 4 o'clock in the morning. My regular customers would always bring the empty half-pint bottles back. By my selling the liquor in half-pint bottles, I made a nice profit. Like I said, this was nothing I was proud of doing. It's just that I needed the money for school.

A year or so later, misfortune came to me and my family. You see, there was a big forest fire that came from the woods near what's now known as Interstate 95. That fire not only burnt down my father's house, but it burnt down my little house too. I lost some songs I had written and a lot of old 78 rpm records. Those records were vintage. After the houses burnt down, my father had a very good friend who offered to help rebuild. That friend's name was Harry Tyrrell.

Even though Mr. Tyrrell was a White man and my father a Black man, they were like brothers. I was always glad to see Mr. and Mrs. Tyrrell come to our house on

Saturday mornings. On those mornings, the Tyrrells would pull up in the yard and pull out boxes of all kinds of items. Some of those items included kitchen utensils, sheets, towels, rolls of wallpaper, toys, clean and freshly starched clothes, and pencils and notebooks for me and my family. Frankly speaking, I don't think I would have finished high school if it hadn't been for the Tyrrells.

My father had occasionally worked for the Tyrrells, who lived further over in Woodbridge. Mr. Tyrrell had an old cinder block house that he had started to build on Featherstone Road. He never finished the house. After Mr. Tyrrell found out that my father's house had burnt down, he told my father that if he could get someone to tear the partially built house down, he could have the cinder blocks, along with the lumber to rebuild. My father accepted Mr. Tyrrell's offer. So, Charles Jr., (Puddin) my oldest brother, had an old 1952 Ford. He, my father, and I made numerous trips in that old 1952 Ford, gathering cinder blocks and lumber from the partially built house that Mr. Tyrrell had given us. We drove that old Ford back and forth from Bethel Road (Smoketown Road) to Featherstone Road. I guess it was about three or four miles each way. It took a while, but my father, with the help of neighboring friends and family members, finally got his house built.

Me and my family will forever be grateful for the Tyrrells. Like I said before, Mr. Tyrrell and my father were like brothers. They respected one another. Mr. Tyrrell would often come by and him and my father would be outside sitting around eating crabs, drinking beer, and chatting away. Sometimes, they even played checkers together. They reminded me of the actors Walter Matthau (whom I met and worked with on a movie in New York many years later) and Jack Lemmon in the movie called *Grumpy Old Men.*

My father, Shack, working on the new house.

Most of the Whites and Colored people that lived on Bethel Road got along quite well. Even the ones that lived in other parts of Woodbridge got along pretty good. We all were like family. We all looked out for one another. It didn't matter if you were Black or White.

Then there were the two White brothers known as the "Bland Brothers" that lived right down the street from where my family lived. The brothers lived on the same side of Bethel Road as my family. Lots of times, when I'd be walking home from the store or school, those brothers saw me. One or the other would always stop me and give me some old comic books, such as *Dick Tracy, Blondie, Westerns, Mutt and Jeff,* etc. They even gave me big, thick catalogues like *Montgomery Ward, Spiegel, Sears and Roebuck,* or *National Bellas Hess.* When my family had a few extra dollars, we'd order the leading Black magazines, like *Ebony* or *Jet.* At the age of 13 or 14, I was a delivery boy for a newspaper called the *Afro-American*. It was a Black newspaper that was started in 1892.

Not far up the road from our house lived an elderly White man by the name of Joe Hedges. He was very tall, well over 6 feet, white hair, and had a long white beard. Whenever I saw him, he always had on old, worn-out, denim overalls with shoulder straps. He reminded me of Rip Van Winkle. Mr. Hedges' house was on the northeast side of Bethel Road, just above where Freedom High School sits today. My family's house was on the west side of the road. Right behind Mr. Hedges house was a cemetery. East of the cemetery was a trailer park, which sat on the northwest side of Route 1, also known as Jefferson Davis Highway.

Old man Joe Hedges owned a lot of peach trees and apple trees. He would let us Colored kids gather some of the fruits when they were ripened. Sometimes, my family would make homemade cider out of the apples. Then there were times when my father would buy the already homemade cider directly from Mr. Hedges. Even though I was young, my father would occasionally let me sample the cider. I liked it. It tasted pretty good. That cider was potent, too. You could get drunk if you drank enough of it. Mr. Hedges also dipped and chewed snuff. He could spit that snuff a mile away. And it always landed right in the container he had placed somewhere on the floor. The more I think of it now, I hope none of that snuff landed in that homemade cider. If it did, it sure was good.

Besides owning numerous fruit trees, including pear trees, Mr. Hedges owned a lot of chickens. Whenever my brother Jimmy and I thought Mr. Hedges was asleep or wasn't around, we'd sneak and go steal a chicken and bring it home for cooking. We would take a hatchet or an ax and chop off the chicken's head. The dead, headless chicken would be flipping and flopping all around on the ground. Once it was completely dead, we dipped it up and down in boiling hot water and plucked off the feathers. You see, the boiling hot water made it somewhat easy to remove the feathers. Once the feathers were picked off the chicken, the next step was to cut the chicken so we could take out all the guts. Once that was done, the chicken was now ready to be cleaned and cooked.

Back during that time, which was in the 1950s, my family ate quite a bit of chicken. There was fried chicken, chicken soup, boiled chicken, and chicken and dumplings. The homemade chicken and dumplings was one of my favorite dishes.

Even though we were on the borderline of being poor, we were never really starving. It was just something that my family went through at the time. Then again, we were not the only ones having a hard time in this part of Woodbridge, especially here on Bethel Road. For example, there was a White family known as the Weeks who lived right up the street from us. Even though the Weeks were White, they were having a rough time too, just like us Coloreds. The Weeks and us Coloreds got along very well. Both families would visit one another and became close-knit. We often referred to each other as "cousins." We, too, were like family. It was rumored that the Weeks were related to some of the Coloreds here in Woodbridge. All of us, whether you were White or Colored, were just trying to make ends meet. We had to make do of what we had. After all, it was the 1950s and rough times were upon us.

My sister Doris (Sis) and her daughters and granddaughter.

Me at my father's rebuilt house.

# BEYOND KANKEY HILL

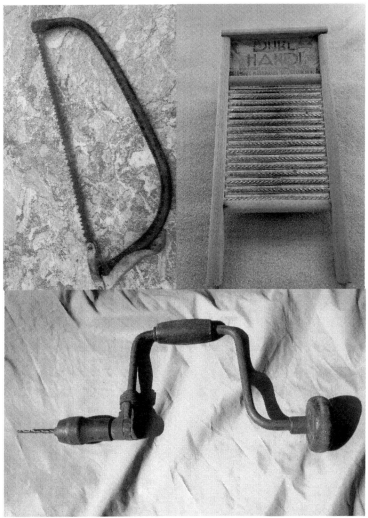

Saw and drill my father would use, and washboard my Sis used.

Blackberry bushes we would pick from as children.

# CHAPTER 2
# School Days

I was quite old when I first started school. I believe I was 7 or 8 years old. My mother died in 1943, and I never knew her. My father had kept me from going to school because he didn't want me walking a long way to catch a school bus. The walk from home to the bus stop was about two miles. Walking that distance also meant that I had to walk along the side of Jefferson Davis Highway (also known as Route 1), which always had a lot of traffic. Somehow, I would make that walk every day to get to the bus stop.

The old elementary school I went to was called Cabin Branch School and was located on Mine Road in Dumfries, Virginia. The school had an old potbelly stove that used coal for heating. In the wintertime, no matter how many layers of clothes you put on, you would still be cold. Seems like my feet always stayed cold. A lot of my shoes had holes in the bottom. Whenever it rained, I would wrap my feet in plastic left over from the dry cleaners. Not only did the plastic keep my feet dry, but it helped keep in some of the warmth. I would be so cold at times that my entire body ached all over. Sometimes, the school bus wouldn't have any heat at all. Yet, we Colored children rode that cold bus to school five days a week.

In front of the school was an old-fashion water pump, which had a tin handle dipper attached to it. In order to get water from the pump, you had to pump it until the water came up from the ground. All the teachers and students drank out of the same dipper.

One of the most memorable things that stood out at Cabin Branch School was the month of May. It was the month when at its beginning, all the boys had to wear a white shirt, black pants, and a black necktie. The girls had to wear a white dress and black shoes. The teachers would gather all the children and lead them to the flagpole, which had many strings of rope dangling downward from the top. The children would grab a string and walk around the flagpole, which some of us called the "May Pole." It was the celebration of springtime, and it was quite a sight to see. When I got home from school, I would eat supper and do my homework. We didn't have electricity, so I would lie on the floor and do my homework by the light coming from an old kerosene-burning lamp.

Kerosene lamp.

After spending a few years at Cabin Branch School, a new elementary school opened in Dumfries, Virginia, and I started attending that school. The school was called Washington Reid Elementary School. It went up to the 8$^{th}$ grade. Nothing had changed much by the time I started the 9$^{th}$ grade at a high school in Manassas. The name of the high school I attended was called Manassas Regional High School. However, when it was first founded by Jennie Dean in 1894, it was called Manassas Industrial School for Colored Youths. By the time I graduated, the name of the school was changed to its original founder's name, Jennie Dean High School. Jennie Dean had been a slave but was freed by the Emancipation Proclamation Act of 1863. Miss Dean wanted a school where Colored youths could learn a trade. The school offered such courses as Home Economics, Barbering, Cosmetology, Carpentry, and Academics. I took classes in Carpentry, Barbering, Chemistry, Algebra, Biology, and other Academics.

Some of the books I used were used books donated to Jennie Dean High School from a nearby White school called Osbourn High School. I particularly remember my used Biology book that had been donated to the school. The book was old, soiled, and very raggedy. It was so raggedy that the pages were about to fall out. I liked Biology, but I hated carrying that book. Yet, it served its purpose. I was able to learn from it.

While attending high school, there were some sports I participated in, too. I played tennis, baseball, and was on the football team. Even though I was on the football team, the coach, Mr. Ellis, kept me on the bench most of the time. I believe he did that because I was the smallest guy on the team. Whenever he did put me in the game, the game would be almost over. I even tried singing in the school's choir, playing the trombone, and acting in the theatre group.

Because the school was in Manassas, Virginia, the other neighboring Coloreds kids and I still had to make that long walk down Bethel Road onto Jefferson Davis Highway in order to catch the school bus. Garfield High School, which was a school for Whites, was in walking distance from where me and the other Colored kids lived. The Jim Crow laws of that time, the 1950s and early 1960s, prevented us Coloreds from going to any of the White schools. All we Colored kids wanted was to get an education. I liked going to school, despite the mistreatment by some White kids and the harsh elements of the weather. I remember White kids riding on their school bus and making fun of us Colored kids as we walked along the road or highway. White kids would pull the windows down on their bus, spit at us, stick their tongues out at us, and make all kinds of racial epithets towards us.

One morning on our way to catch the school bus, one of the boys in our Colored group of kids did something that I will never forget. When we got down to Jefferson Davis Highway, the Colored boy crossed over the highway to the east side where there was a little country store called Doc Hampton's Log Cabin Store. The boy went in the store and brought some candies, such as Mary Jane, Tootsie Rolls, and a few other penny candies, which were all put in a little brown bag. After the boy received the bag of candy, he returned to the west side of Jefferson Davis where the Colored kids were still walking in route to catch the school bus. The boy emptied the bag of candy into his pant pockets. He then went behind some bushes off the highway and peed in the brown paper bag. When the school bus came by with the White kids on it, the Colored boy threw that bag of pee right in the face of one of those White kids. After that incident, those White kids never did pull that school bus window down again. But they did continue with their racial epithets, making faces, and sticking tongues out at us.

After Grandma Ora Bell died in 1955, the following year (1956), Sis and her children, along with me, moved from Bethel Road into Grandma's house. It was located on what's now known as Cardinal Drive. The house had two floors. In order to get to the second floor, one had to walk up a long stairway of steps extending upward, similar to the stairways in the old Dutch houses in the Netherlands. Although the house was equipped with electricity, there was no running water. We got our water from a well and a nearby spring. Because the house had no indoor plumbing, we had to use an outhouse. For all those who don't know what an outhouse is, it's an outdoor toilet. After I turned 18, I moved back to Smoketown Road to live with my father.

When I was about to graduate from Jennie Dean High School in 1961, I was offered a scholarship for four years to attend Virginia Union University in Richmond, Virginia. I didn't take the offer because I didn't want to go farther south than Woodbridge. Instead, I opted to go to Howard University in Washington, DC. Both schools are historical Black schools. So, in September of 1961, I moved to Washington, DC, and lived with my aunt Nettie Bell. Her house was located at 736 Newton Place NW, Washington, DC, and was in walking distance from Howard University. I was glad of that closeness because that meant I wouldn't have to take public transportation to get to school.

# ALBERT J. WILLIAMS

My high school graduation picture from 1961.

There were two floors in Aunt Nettie's house, and it had a very tiny back yard. The second floor consisted of two small bedrooms, two small closets, and a small bathroom off from the foyer. She rented out one of the bedrooms to a boarder. I stayed in the other bedroom. The boarder was an elderly, tall, dark-skin Black man, who kept to himself. I didn't see him that much, other than occasionally passing him when I was going to work or coming home from school. I had already started full-time day classes at Howard, and I took on a full-time night janitorial job at the FHA (Federal Housing Administration) in downtown Washington, DC. Going to school full time during the day and working full time at night was rough. I mean *rough*. I know, because I did it.

Anyhow, one Saturday morning as I was sitting at the kitchen table eating my breakfast, the boarder came down the stairs and saw me. He said to me, "Good morning. I have two tickets to the Senators ball game for this afternoon. You wanna go?" I said, "Sure. Love baseball." I really did like baseball. I played it when I was in high school. I told Aunt Nettie that I was going to go to the ball game with the boarder. I don't know what she said or if she said anything at all. That afternoon, me and the boarder, whom I believe was a "numbers runner," went to the ball game. The reason I say that about him being a numbers runner is because most times, whenever I saw him, he had a bunch of numbers written on a slip of paper in his hand. They were called "street numbers," and it was illegal to play them. But people played them anyhow. Now days, people play the Lottery numbers, which is legal, but similar to the old way of playing the illegal numbers. What a mess.

The ball game was very boring and the temperature was extremely hot that day. Not only that, we were seated so high up in the stadium that one could barely see the game. We were up there with the pigeons. I was glad when the game was over. When we got home, the old man went upstairs and I went into the kitchen to fix a sandwich. As I was sitting down eating my sandwich, out of nowhere in pops Aunt Nettie. With her hands on her hips, she stands in the doorway. She says to me, "Albert, what are you studying at Howard?" I said, "I'm studying theatre and acting." What she said next really kind of hurt my feelings. She looked at me and said, "Well, you're building castles and they're going to fall on you." I thought that was very nasty of her to say that to me. I believe when I went to the ball game that day, she went upstairs and saw my report card lying on the desk in my room. My report card listed all the courses I was taking at Howard. The report card listed such courses as Acting, Theatre, Fencing, Sociology, Speech, and English. Aunt Nettie went on to say, "Why don't you take up something like accounting or medicine, instead of that *acting* stuff? Take up something more reasonable." I didn't answer her. She turned and walked away. She had ruined my appetite. I don't even think I finished eating my sandwich. Though I must say that years later, when I no longer lived with her, she would go around bragging about me. She would tell people such things as, "Oh, my nephew is an actor and he be on a lot of shows coming out of New York. He's always on the soap operas." That was Aunt Nettie for you.

Another time, when I was still living with her, she showed rudeness towards me. It was on a Sunday morning when we were walking to church. She turns to me and says, "Take your hands out your pockets. Use your head for more than a hat rack." I said to myself, "She did it again. Insulted me." She could be very nasty at times.

Then there were times she would be very kind. I remember one time, when she was in a good mood, she and I were sitting at the dining room table just chatting. She went and got an old shoe box full of black and white pictures. She started pulling out all sorts of pictures and telling me who was who. Most of the people in the pictures were relatives of ours. However, I remember one picture in particular. It was a picture of Aunt Nettie and Mrs. Eleanor Roosevelt, along with other guests, seated at a long table. It appeared to have been a formal dinner party. The guests were all well dressed and seemed to be happy. Mrs. Roosevelt was smiling and Aunt Nettie looked very stern and stoic. Aunt Nettie, pointing at the picture of Mrs. Roosevelt, told me that Mrs. Roosevelt was a very dear friend of hers. I had one family member, who's deceased now, (as is Aunt Nettie), tell me that, yes, Aunt Nettie and Mrs. Roosevelt were good friends. Some people said it was more than just friendship. I don't know. But I do know Mrs. Roosevelt was good to the Colored people. Take for example how she treated the DAR (Daughters of the American Revolution) in 1939. The DAR wouldn't allow Marian Anderson, who was a great opera singer that happened to be Colored, sing at Constitutional Hall. Mrs. Roosevelt boycotted the DAR and went on to be very instrumental in getting Marian Anderson to sing at the steps of the Lincoln Memorial in 1939. It was there that over 70,000 people saw and heard this great operatic singer. To me, Mrs. Roosevelt was a civil rights icon and a fighter for civil rights way before President Lyndon Baines Johnson signed the Civil Rights Act of 1964. I will say, though, while I was staying with Aunt Nettie, I never knew of her visiting Mrs. Roosevelt or Mrs. Roosevelt visiting Aunt Nettie.

 I went on to finish one full year of studying at Howard in June of 1962. At that time, I knew I didn't want to stay with Aunt Nettie anymore. Even though I loved her, she was way too controlling for me. When I told her I was moving back to Virginia, she didn't appear to be surprised at all. I think she may have had a feeling that I wasn't happy living there with her. I quit my job at the FHA and moved back to Woodbridge, Virginia, to live with my father. When I got home, the first thing he asked me was could I shave him. Seems like whenever I would come home, my father always wanted me to shave him. I didn't mind. My father had been very good to me. It was always an honor to shave him.

A few weeks after returning to Woodbridge, I got a job at Alexandria National Bank on King Street in Alexandria, Virginia. I was hired as a Coin Machine Operator and placed in a very small room that couldn't have been no more than 5 feet by 6 feet. There were no windows in the room, just a small door for entering and exiting. My job was to place bags of coins inside the coin counter machine. The machine separated the coins so they could exit into various canvas bags. Pennies went in bags for $50, nickels in bags for $200, quarters in bags for $500, and so on. I would seal the bags and prepare them for shipment to the Federal Reserve Bank in Richmond, Virginia. The job was not difficult. In fact, I liked the job. No one bothered me. The only thing I didn't like was the smallness of the room. It reminded me of a mausoleum.

I worked, saved up a little money, and brought myself a car. I don't know who sold me that car. But I do know it was a 1957 Ford Fairlane 500 painted yellow. I couldn't stand the color yellow on the car. Earl Scheib Paint Shop was running ads advertising $99 paint jobs. I took that car to Earl Scheib Paint Shop located in Alexandria and had the car painted burgundy.

At the time, I was dating a girl named Thelma, who lived in Manassas. She was very petite and shorter than me. I guess she stood about 5 feet 5 inches. I was 5 feet 7 inches. On weekends, I would pick her up in my nice-looking, shiny, 1957 burgundy Ford car and we would go to baseball games in Woodbridge, Dumfries, or Fairfax. All those places had Colored baseball teams. The teams would compete against one another. Mainly, the games gave the Coloreds something to do on the weekends.

When Thelma and I weren't going to the ball games on the weekends, we would go to the movies. We often went to the outdoor drive-in theatre in Manassas. She and I would cozy up and watch the movie on the big outdoor movie screen. Just before the movie started, I would go to the concession stand and get us some snacks and drinks. The concession stand had all kinds of candy goodies, drinks, and popcorn. Near the concession stand, two things stood out that I will never forget. Entrance to one of the two bathrooms had a sign over the door that read, "Whites Only." Entrance to the other bathroom had a sign over the door that read, "For Coloreds." That sign "Coloreds" threw me off. It baffled me. I guess if the Whites wanted to use the Coloreds bathroom, they could. But the Coloreds couldn't use the bathroom for the "Whites Only." I believed that's what the signs meant.

The drive-in theatre was not the only theatre that was segregated in Manassas. There was a theatre on Center Street where Coloreds could go see movies. The only thing was that the Coloreds had to sit upstairs in the balcony and the Whites downstairs. Around 1958 or 1959, a few years before I started dating Thelma, I often went to a theatre down in Occoquan, Virginia. The theatre was called Lyric and it sat right off the Occoquan River. That theatre, too, was segregated. Coloreds had to sit upstairs and Whites downstairs. The theatre was always cold. I guess because it was so close to the water. I remember water rats running near my feet while I watched movies. Seemed like I was always looking down at the floor for rats more than I looked at the movie screen. The last movie I saw at the Lyric was a movie made and released in 1954. The movie was called *On the Waterfront*, and it starred a young actor by the name of Marlon Brando.

Getting back to Thelma, she wanted to get married, but I wanted to further my education. In the back of my head were thoughts of going into the Army. I figured that if I went into the military, I could go to school on the GI Bill when I got out. I began to do some serious thinking as to what were my long-term plans for life.

# CHAPTER 3
# March On Washington August 28, 1963

During the spring and early part of the summer of 1963, I had been hearing on the radio about a planned civil rights march in the making. The news was that there was going to be thousands of people demanding jobs, freedom, and racial equality descending on Washington, DC, on August 28, 1963. I got in touch with the local NAACP (National Association for the Advancement of Colored People) and spoke with its president, Mr. James Russell. I asked him if the NAACP was going to the march. He answered, "yes," and that if I wanted a ride, I could ride with him. I thanked him and agreed to take that ride. As a man of color and having experienced discrimination here in Prince William County, I wanted to be a part of that march. I just had to be.

The night before the march, I made a sign that read "Freedom Now." I was looking forward to going to that march. On the morning of the march, around 8 a.m., Mr. Russell pulled up in the yard. He was driving an old white van. I don't know what year or make of the van. There was another gentleman sitting in the front on the passenger's side. I assumed he was a member of the NAACP. I got in the back seat of the van, along with my homemade sign. I was very excited. I believe we got to Washington, DC, around 9 a.m., or close to it. Everywhere you looked were cars, trucks, and people. Fourteenth Street and Constitution Avenue were lined up with ambulances, rescue squads, and fire trucks. The city of Washington, DC, was ready.

The organizers had called for a peaceful march. A. Philip Randolph and Bayard Rustin were the main organizers. But you don't hear much about them. (In August of 2022, I was cast as a United Auto Worker in an upcoming Netflix movie called *Rustin*).

A traffic officer directed us to a parking spot right off Constitutional Avenue. The three of us, Mr. Russell, the gentleman in the front seat, and me, somehow made our way close to the reflecting pool facing the Washington Monument. We were in the middle of the huge crowd of people. Everywhere you looked were people. They were up on the lampposts, on the iron rails, on top of cars and trucks, and even in the trees. As the day proceeded, the temperature must have reached over 100 degrees by noon. People were wringing wet with sweat. Some were passing out, most likely from the heat. I particularly remember a young White girl, must had been in her early or mid-twenties, being pushed up in the air by people in the crowd. We had our hands extended upward passing her along to the rescue squad so she could get some help. I think the heat was just too much for her.

Quite a few dignitaries spoke before Rev. Martin Luther King, Jr. spoke. There were prayers, singing, and more speeches. All of a sudden, from the direction of the Lincoln Memorial, I heard a deep singing voice filling the air. It was the voice of the world-renowned gospel singer Mahalia Jackson. She sung "Take My Hand Precious Lord." I had been told that Rev. King had requested she sing that particular song. As Mahalia was singing, chills rolled through my body. I really don't know how to explain it. It was an innate feeling that I got at the time.

People in the crowd were saying, "Amen," "Yes Lord," "Hallelujah," and "Sing Mahalia, Sing." The whole scene was spectacular.

I felt that this is what America is about: unity, respect, and love. But my Lord, when Rev. Martin Luther King, Jr. got up there at that podium and spoke, the crowd went crazy, in a good way. It was like being at a Sunday morning Baptist Church service. At the end of Rev. King's speech, I got a little teary eyed when he said, "Free at last, free at last. Thank God Almighty, we are free at last." But I felt even better when all the people joined hands and sung "We Shall Overcome." I walked out of that march feeling elated because I saw for myself that Black folks, White folks, and all other folks can come together. I believed it then and I believe it now. It was amazing to see so many people of different races and ethnic backgrounds together on this day, a day of reckoning. There was no looting, no burning, no rioting, or anything of that nature. It was a peaceful demonstration. The press stated that over 250,000 people attended that march. I say it was more like 500,000 or more.

Afterwards, Mr. Russell and the man in the front passenger's seat, and I, made our way through the crowd to the van. Mr. Russell dropped me off at my home in Woodbridge, and I thanked him for taking me to that awesome event. It had been a day I will never forget. The next day after the March on Washington, I went back to my job at the Alexandria National Bank. It was getting close to September. I wanted to go back to school but didn't have the money. September and October came and went.

Though I have no pictures from that August day, the following are pictures of me attending the Million Man March in DC on October 16, 1995.

Me at the Million Man March in DC on October 16, 1995.

The Million Man March in DC on October 16, 1995.

## CHAPTER 4
## The Army Life

At the beginning of November 1963, I went to the Military Recruiting Office in Manassas to find out how to enlist in the Army. I filled out some papers and was told to contact the Armed Forces Service Department in Maryland. I believe that department was in Hyattsville, Maryland. I called them and was given a date to come in for an interview. My brother Puddin drove me to Maryland on November 25, 1963. That day, I had planned on *volunteering* for the Army. Coincidentally, I ended up being drafted on that same day. I took a written test, had a physical exam, and was sworn in under oath to be in the United States Army. All that happened three days after President John F. Kennedy was assassinated on Friday, November 22, 1963. In my mind, I could hear President Kennedy saying, "Ask not what your country can do for you. Ask what you can do for your country." I was now a soldier. I told my brother to go home and that I would get in touch with him. I also told him to tell my sister, Sis, to keep my car for me until I got out of the Army.

The next day after the new recruits were sworn in, we stood in line and waited for our names to be called to find out where we were going for basic training. When my name was called, I was assigned to Fort Jackson, South Carolina. That afternoon, about 10 or 15 of us new soldiers went via an Army military envoy to Fort Jackson, which was nicknamed Tar Heel. Why it was called that, I really don't know. I had heard and read somewhere that it had something to do with slavery and the confederacy. I spent eight weeks at Fort Jackson doing my basic military training. My advanced training was to be done at Fort Ord, California.

To get to California, I took an Amtrak train from Fort Jackson, South Carolina, out to California. The train ride was wonderful. I had a sleeping car, which had a bunk bed and a small wash basin. The train also had something called a "dome car," which was made out of glass. You could sit in that car, look out through the dome, and see mountains, rivers, the desert, and everything. En route to California from South Carolina, I saw lots of great scenery. I'll tell anyone that if you want to see America and all its beauty, take a train ride across this great country. You will find out that you don't need to leave America to see beauty. We have it all right here.

When I got to Fort Ord, California, I was assigned to the Ordinance Supply Unit. Its main objective was to supply linen and various military items to the soldiers. Besides the physical training, which was more intense than the basic training at Fort Jackson, I survived the advanced training at Fort Ord. Working in the supply unit, my assignment was to give towels, washcloths, sheets, and pillowcases to the soldiers whenever they needed those items. I was only a PFC (Private First Class). The sergeant that was in charge of the supply room treated me okay. Most of the time when he came to work, he looked a little drunk. But that was none of my business.

One day when I was alone sitting at my desk, in comes the colonel. Big man. Four stars. Must have been 6 feet 7 inches. Around 250 lbs. Looked like a Paul Bunyan. He says to me, "Private Williams." I jumped to attention until he gave me the "at ease" command. "I need two sheets, two pillowcases, and a few towels and washcloths." He made that request on more than one occasion. But I would always give him what he requested and then he would leave. Ten or fifteen minutes later, I'd look out the window and see the colonel and his secretary leaving their office. It was rumored that they were going together. She was not a bad-looking woman. Very bosomy and voluptuous. She had a full head of white hair. She looked a little like the movie star Jayne Mansfield from the 1956 movie *The Girl Can't Help It*. While I worked in supply, I noticed that the colonel and his secretary had their little rendezvous more than once. But whatever they did was none of my business. I joined the Army to serve my country. Nothing more, nothing less.

Me in the supply room at Fort Ord, California, 1964.

In 1964, I came home on a leave of absence for 30 days, known as a furlough. I took an Army prop plane (a plane used for transporting military cargo) from California to Andrews Air Force Base in Maryland. The plane ride was rough. Because I was a soldier, and the plane was bringing military equipment to Maryland, I didn't have to pay anything. I was decked out in my military uniform and was lucky to catch a free ride. From Andrews Air Force Base, I took a Greyhound bus to Washington, DC, and then to Woodbridge. I was glad to be home.

I spent some time with Thelma, who wasn't so pushy about getting married as she was just before I went in the Army. Maybe she had found someone else. I didn't question her. I really enjoyed spending time with my family. Of course, I had to shave my dad. The 30 days went by so fast. Next thing I knew, I was on a plane heading back to California.

When I got to Fort Ord, my sergeant told me that I had orders for Vietnam, but that the colonel somehow got me out of them. Was it because of the sheets, towels, and pillowcases? I guess I will never know. Anyhow, the entire army base was to participate in an exercise military event called Exercise Desert Strike. My unit, the Ordinance Supply Unit, was one of the many participants. The event took place in the Mojave Desert where all three states, California, Arizona, and Nevada, connect. Most of the time, the temperature was near one hundred degrees or higher. At the same time, soldiers could look up in the direction of the mountains and see snow. Yet, guys were passing out in the desert from heat exhaustion.

Besides having to deal with the excessive heat, we had to deal with scorpions. None of us wanted to be stung by those creatures. The Exercise Desert Strike was tough and rough. The entire exercise lasted for about two months. When we finished, all of us soldiers were glad and went back to the base at Fort Ord. I was put in charge of my barracks, which housed about 25 or 30 guys. They slept out in the open on single or double bunk beds. Even though it was small, I had my own private room. I didn't mind being in charge of the barracks. It was just that I really didn't like telling people what to do. Though I did my best.

Most of the guys were new recruits. Many times, I would have a card game in my room. Guys would come in and we would play Blackjack. I was *always* the dealer. Guys would lose their money and borrow money from me until they got paid. If they borrowed twenty dollars, they had to pay me back twenty-five dollars. The more they borrowed, the more they had to pay me back. I guess you could call me a loan shark. When payday came around, the guys always paid me back without complaining.

If we had a day off and some free time, some of us would visit the clubhouse on base and have a few beers. Other times we'd go into the two nearby towns: Seaside or Monterey. It was more fun going into town. The town of Seaside had a wharf known for its seafood. It served some of the best seafood I've ever had in my life. Neither had I ever seen such huge crabs. They looked like something out of a horror movie. Seaside, California, was nice, but I think I liked Monterey, California, better. Monterey was known for its annual Monterey Jazz Festival. Once a year, jazz musicians from all over the world would congregate at this great jazz festival. There was one little cute jazz club in Monterey that I really liked going to in the evenings. I would often go there whenever I was off duty. I don't recall the name of the club, but the ambiance and music was very good.

There was a very attractive barmaid that worked at the club. She had jet-black hair and was of French descent. Every time I walked in the club, seemed liked her eyes would light up. So did mine. I liked her and I think she liked me. She often gave me free drinks. One time, the jukebox was playing "My Girl," a song by the Temptations. I looked at her and said, "That song is from me to you." She smiled and gave me another free drink.

My Army photo in 1963.

Before I knew it, time had creeped up on me. It was time to get back to the military base. We GIs had to be back on base by a certain time.

One weekend, when I didn't have any Army details and was off duty, my best buddy, James, asked me if I wanted to ride down to L.A. (Los Angeles) with him for the weekend. He rented a car and I agreed to ride with him. It was a beautiful ride along the Pacific Palisades of the Pacific Ocean. We rode about 17 miles on the Palisades before getting on the freeways. Altogether, it took us over two hours to get to L.A. When we arrived, I was introduced to his wife, Betty. As we all started talking, I noticed a lot of liquor and wine bottles on the kitchen table. James, pointing towards the kitchen table, asked his wife where did she get all that stuff. Her reply to him was that she got it from the riots. In other words, she had gotten that stuff as a result of the Watts Riots, which were over with before James and I got to L.A. The Watts Riots lasted from August 11, 1965 to August 16, 1965. Thirty-four people lost their lives in that riot. Because my buddy and I were only going to be in L.A. for the weekend, we left on that Sunday afternoon and headed back to Fort Ord. But before leaving L.A., we rode through Watts. All you could see was burnt-out buildings, ash, ruined furniture, and clothing. It was a sad sight to see. Some of the items destroyed still showed signs of smoke.

 When we got back to the base at Fort Ord, it was Army business as usual, such as combat training, KP (kitchen patrol), and guard duty. The month of August was about to end. Fall was close by and I really had to do some serious thinking of my future. When I got drafted for the Army in November of 1963, it was to be for two years of active duty and four years of inactive duty. November 1965 was to be the month for my discharge of active duty. I kept asking myself if I was going to re-enlist in the Army or leave? Time seemed like it was moving so fast. In October, I was promoted to Corporal First Class. I guess that was an incentive to get me to re-enlist. However, I decided to leave the Army. When November of 1965 came, I was Honorably Discharged for Honest and Faithful Service to the United States of America. I had done my two years of active duty and would serve four years of inactive duty. If I had to serve in the military again, I would do it in a heartbeat.

I told my closest comrades that I had decided not to re-enlist, and that I was leaving and would keep in touch with them. They all wished me well. The day of my departure, one of the soldiers was going to San Francisco and said he could drop me off at San Francisco Airport. I was able to get a flight out of San Francisco to Washington National Airport. Once there, I took a cab from the airport to the bus station in DC. The next bus out of DC going to Woodbridge was a very long wait time, about six or seven hours. However, there was an earlier Greyhound bus heading to Richmond, Virginia, passing Woodbridge but stopping in Triangle. I decided to take that bus because Triangle was only a few miles south of Woodbridge. When I got to Triangle, I took a cab home to live with my father. We were glad to see each other. Yes, I had to shave him. His beard had gotten whiter. We spent time together and I visited family members and friends. At the time, I didn't look for a job because I had been thinking about moving to New York.

December came and, of course, there was the Christmas holiday. I gave my father some shirts, socks, gloves, and a few other gifts that I thought he could use (like a shaving set). He gave me a couple of twenty-dollar bills and told me to get myself something for Christmas. Exactly how much money he gave me, I don't know. I had already told him I was moving to New York. He wanted to know what was I going to be doing in New York. I told him I wanted to get a job, go to school, and live there for a while. He didn't seem too pleased. But he did say, "If you need anything, let me know. You be careful up there." I thanked him. It was a very sad moment.

Me (bottom right) with GI friends and comrades.

Me in the Army at Ford Ord, 1965.

# CHAPTER 5
# Moving To New York

On January 6, 1966, I boarded a Greyhound bus from Woodbridge to New York City. All I had with me were a few pieces of clothing tucked in my Army duffel bag, a shopping bag with some items, and less than a hundred dollars in my pockets. When I arrived at New York City's Port Authority a little before midnight, I got off the Greyhound bus and went inside. I put my duffel bag and the shopping bag in two different lockers. I believe the cost was 25 cents per locker. I felt some type of release, but I knew my biggest challenges were ahead of me.

I started walking on 42$^{nd}$ Street, known as the Times Square area. I was in awe. Oh, the splendor of all the bright lights. Wow! Neon lights were everywhere I looked. There were so many huge buildings, and yes, many people were out walking the streets at that early hour in the morning. I knew I had to find some place to live. I walked around the Times Square area for a while but couldn't find any vacant rooms for rent. I started walking north towards Central Park, Columbus Circle, and Amsterdam Avenue. I still didn't see any "rooms for rent" signs. I walked up and down those side streets in Manhattan so many times that morning. My feet were killing me. I spent hours trying to find a place where I could rent a room. I decided I'd try walking north on a street called Broadway. That street had a lot of exquisite-looking shops and boutiques. Street vendors were selling food on the street, even at this early hour in the morning, which was about 5 a.m. There were great-looking buildings, such as the Lincoln Center for the Performing Arts and The Juilliard Music School. I was still walking north when I saw a sign that read $94^{th}$ street. I turned east on $94^{th}$ street and walked towards the Hudson River, which is the river that divides New York from New Jersey. Continuing to walk east, I could see Hoboken, New Jersey, on the other side of the Hudson River. Running parallel with the river is the Westside Highway and Riverside Drive. The lights on the New Jersey side were bright, but not as bright as the lights on New York's side.

On Riverside Drive, I spotted a big hotel with a sign in the window advertising "Rooms for Rent." I go inside the hotel, which was called Riverside Hotel. There's an elderly White lady behind the desk and I say, "Good morning." She says, "Good morning. What can I do for you?" I told her that I needed a room for a few days. She went on to tell me that the rooms were $13.00 a night. I asked her if the room had a refrigerator, stove, and bath. Her reply to me was the room had none of that. However, she did tell me there was a bathroom and a shower on the floor, and everyone on that floor could use both. I thanked her and paid her for two nights in advance. She gave me the key and told me to take the elevator to the third floor. The room was very small and faced a dark-gray brick wall. After examining the room for a while, I had to go back downtown to Port Authority to get my stuff out of the lockers. It was now close to 6 a.m.

The streets were beginning to show huge crowds hustling and bustling to get to work or to wherever. It was almost like being in a circus. I retrieved all my items from the lockers and boarded a transit bus going back north on Broadway to $94^{th}$ street. I was glad to get back to the hotel. When I put the key in the slot and opened the door, I was greeted by a few unwanted guests. *Holy Moses! Cockroaches!* "Oh well," I said to myself, "I have to live somewhere." I took my shoes off and blisters were all over the bottom of my feet. At the front desk sat the little old German lady, who was very pleasant and had dark red hair, similar to actress Lucille Ball. The front desk lady was actually the manager of the hotel. After two or three days, I went out to look for a job.

The first place I went to was First National City Bank at 399 Park Avenue near the Bloomingdale's store. The location is considered the wealthy upper eastside of Manhattan. I got the job the same day. I was hired as a clerk. All I did all day was stuff envelopes, known as proxies. The people were nice to work with, but the job was very boring. I was paid the minimum wage, and after taxes, I took home about $85 a week. Receiving that $85 was like receiving a million dollars. The first thing I did was pay the manager of the hotel where I stayed. I always paid my rent on time and often paid in advance. One time, the manager told me that I looked like Sammy Davis, Jr. Ha! I laughed. Whenever I went out and she was at her desk, she would smile, and I'd smile right back at her.

After I paid my rent, I walked to the Woolworth store and brought a hot plate, a knife, a fork, paper plates and a few other things. Now, while staying at the hotel, I could at least heat up a can of beans or Vienna Sausage. I stayed at that hotel less than three weeks. Eventually, I found an apartment in the Bronx. The building was an old pre-war building. Built solid. The apartment had three nice, spacious rooms and overlooked Crotona Park. On weekends, that park would be crowded with families cooking out, playing games, and sunbathing. The subway was nearby, and that made it easier for me to get around in

New York, especially commuting back and forth to my job at First National City Bank downtown.

One day during my lunch break, I saw an ad in the *New York Times* that said the Federal Reserve Bank of New York (FRBNY) was hiring Coin Machine Operators. I knew I had the experience because of my previous job at the Alexandria National Bank in Virginia before I moved to New York. So, I asked my supervisor could I take an extended lunch hour to take care of some personal business. She said that it was okay. I went to the $59^{th}$ street subway station and took the downtown train to Wall Street. The ride took about half an hour. Once I got to the Federal Reserve Bank of New York, the guard showed me how to get to the Personnel Department for my interview. Once there, I took a written exam and was told that someone would be contacting me soon. I thanked the interviewer, rushed back to the subway train going uptown north, and went back to work at First National City Bank.

A few days later I got a call from the Federal Reserve Bank of New York asking me when could I come in and take a physical. I went in the next day right after I got off from work. Within a week's time, I was hired. On February 1, 1967, I started working as a Coin Machine Operator at the Federal Reserve Bank of New York (and later retired from on February 1, 1995). Still living in my Bronx apartment and having a new job, I felt very good.

I've always been an avid reader of newspapers. One Saturday morning when I was reading the *New York Times*, I saw an ad advertising an apartment for rent on Bank Street, which is an affluent area known as Greenwich Village in lower Manhattan. I called the listed phone number and asked if I could come and see the apartment. The guy that answered the phone said that I could come anytime that night after 11 p.m. or Monday. I told him I could come there that night after 11 p.m. In the back of my head I was thinking that time may be too late. However, he said that it was okay to come at that time. Therefore, a little before 11 p.m., I boarded the subway train in the Bronx and headed downtown to Bank Street. I got there a little before midnight and walked to 119 Bank Street.

It was a lovely area with beautiful brownstones, tree-lined streets, and cobblestone sidewalks. One could tell it was an upper-class neighborhood. The congresswoman Bella Abzug (who fought for equal rights for all) also lived on Bank Street. I used to see her leaving her brownstone home. The apartment I went to see was on the third floor and in a walkup building. There was no elevator. As I knocked on the door, some guy with long black hair opened the door and introduced me to his lady friend. She was very attractive and also had long black hair. The way the two of them were dressed, I assumed they were hippies. After all, it was the 60s. It was a time when many people were in the "hippie zone." Anyhow, the apartment was very small. The floors were lopsided, and no two people could be in the kitchen at the same time. There was a non-working fireplace. Outside the window was a fire escape facing the back of a brick building. I believe the couple was asking $65 or $75 a month. I told them I wanted the apartment and gave them a down payment. How much of a down payment, I really don't know. They said that I could move in the next Saturday and pay the balance of the rent at that time. When Saturday came, I went back down to Bank Street, paid the couple the balance, and took possession of that apartment. We all wished each other the best. I ended up staying in that apartment nearly ten years.

Me working in the back yard of my 119 Bank Street apartment.

In fact, I was still living in that apartment when one of the biggest musical festivals took place. It was known as Woodstock. The location was in a little town called Bethel, New York. I remember the event quite well. Four of my closest friends and I piled into a small Volkswagen on that Friday night of August 1969 and headed to upstate New York to a camping resort. It was raining like cats and dogs. Traffic was terrible. The closer we got upstate, traffic and rain got worse. There were people half naked walking along the New York Thruway. They were wringing wet from all the rain. The traffic was at a standstill for hours. We got out of the car to stretch our legs for a few minutes. The people were very friendly. We could hear the music coming from the direction of the festival. We got out of the car and started to walk in the direction of the music. Because it was raining so hard and mud was everywhere, we decided to get back in the car and continue on our journey. Sounded like I heard the American folk singer Richie Havens singing the song "Freedom." When my friends and I got back in the car, we were finally able to drive to Monticello, New York, which was our destination. We spent the rest of that weekend in Monticello and headed back to New York City that Sunday afternoon.

Once we got back to the city, everyone went their own way. I went back to my apartment on Bank Street, and Monday morning, I went back to work at the bank. The bank had been good to me in helping to pay my tuition for college. While still working during the day at the bank, I was able to take night classes and sometimes a 6 a.m. class at the nearby Pace University. The 6 a.m. class finished at 8 a.m. That allowed me time to get to my 9 a.m. job. With the tuition assistance I got from the bank, and self-determination, I was finally able to get my Bachelor of Arts degree in English and Writing.

However, I must say though, that I felt the bank didn't treat me and other Blacks fairly when it came to promotions. Accordingly, I took it upon myself to institute a discrimination lawsuit against the bank. When I first started working at the Federal Reserve Bank of New York in February of 1967, I had no idea that I would end up suing the bank. I first started complaining of the discrimination at the bank in the late 1970s. The bank had its own internal EEO (Equal Employment Office). I remember going to three different managers of that office and nothing of avail came to my satisfaction. The managers, also known as chiefs, were all people of color. To me, they reminded me of a character in a book called *The Spook Who Sat by the Door*, written by Sam Greenlee. The chiefs were just window dressings.

After I didn't get any positive results from the bank's internal EEO, I decided to go outside of the bank and contacted the EEOC (Equal Employment Opportunity Commission) of New York. I met with a few field officers of that agency but was told to contact Ms. Eleanor Holmes Norton (who was in charge of the EEOC of New York at that time, and currently a Washington, DC, delegate). After my meeting with Ms. Norton, who listened diligently to my complaint and is a brilliant woman, she recommended that I contact the U.S. Equal Employment Opportunity Commission in Washington, DC. The chairman of the office in Washington, DC, was Chairman Clarence Thomas, who is currently one of the Supreme Court nine Justices. I wrote a letter to Mr. Thomas explaining my situation at the FRBNY. In fact, there were many letters written back and forth between me and the EEOC office in Washington, DC.

From an inside source at the FRBNY, I was told that Mr. Thomas's office did send investigators to the bank to investigate my claim of racial discrimination and retaliation. The Affirmative Action Program was very controversial during this time. The same source that told me about investigators coming to the bank also told me that a Haitian woman, who at the time she applied for a job at the FRBNY indicated on her employment application that her race was White. However, after she found out about my complaint to the EEOC and my contacting Mr. Clarence Thomas, the Haitian woman changed her race from White to Black on her personnel records.

I was tired. Not only was I tired, but I was frustrated from going to various meetings, writing letters, and getting negative results. So, I decided to go ahead and file a discrimination lawsuit in the United States District Court

Southern District of New York against the Federal Reserve Bank of New York. In preparing for the lawsuit, I talked with eight or ten other Black employees, trying to get them to join me in a class-action lawsuit. I felt there would be strength in numbers. But lo and behold, they all backed out when it got close to court time. I guess they were afraid of retaliation.

I hired a Jewish attorney and we both worked quite well together. When I told him that I had gone down to the District Court in New York and asked for a certain judge to handle the case, he told me that I should not have done that and that I should have left that up to him. The judge I requested and was assigned had been a former president of New York's office of the NAACP (National Association for the Advancement of Colored People). I thought that the judge, being Black and a past president of the NAACP, would have a better understanding of my case. When the trial started, it lasted nearly a week. I still have a copy of my continued deposition, which took place at 11:15 a.m. on the $22^{nd}$ day of February 1980.

I filed the lawsuit because I felt something had to be done about the racism at the bank. It was very obvious that Blacks were being overlooked for higher paying positions. As for me, when new White guys were hired in my department, I had to train them. Not only did I have some college education behind me, but I was attending night school and studying to get my college degree, which I did get. The White guys I trained had no college degree and were not attending any type of school. What really bothered me was when they got promoted over me. It just wasn't right. It was overt racism. Nothing else. Plain as day.

I didn't win the lawsuit against the bank. However, *I may have lost the fight but I won the war*. The reason I say that is simply because shortly afterwards, Blacks started getting promotions and better positions at the bank. Now, I am no John Lewis, the late, great African American Congressman from the State of Georgia. But like him, I believe that if you see something, say something, do something. Well, I saw something, I said something, and I did something. I sued the Federal Reserve Bank of New York. Congressman Lewis often stated that he "got in good trouble." Well, I can say the same about me now. I got in good trouble. Another thing Congressman Lewis and I had in common was that we both attended the March on Washington on August 28, 1963. He was 23 years old and I was 22.

I finally did get a promotion at the bank. When I got that promotion, I was put in a very small cubicle that contained a computer, a desk, a phone, and other office supplies. The space was about 5 feet by 8 feet. There was a very small opening for entering and exiting (a little larger space than what I had when I was younger and worked at the Alexandria National Bank in Alexandria, Virginia). One day while I was sitting at my desk, an elderly Jewish lady, who had a pretty high position at the bank, came by my cubicle. She peeks inside my cubicle and says, "Oh My Goodness! They put you in a mausoleum!" I had to laugh, but deep down inside of me I was very distraught.

At the bank, I had one supervisor, who was White and extremely good to me. She would let me take extended lunch hours to go into midtown Manhattan to do interviews and auditions. If I had some business to take care of, she would let me leave the job early or come in late. She had seen me on TV and in various movies. I remember showing her my Actor's Union cards and she was very impressed. A few times, when I was going to drive or take Amtrak from New York to Washington, DC, or Virginia, my supervisor would ask me what time I needed to leave. I would tell her and she'd let me leave at the time I requested. She always treated me quite well.

One time when she let me leave early, I went DC to see my sister and my family in Virginia. My sister no longer lived in Virginia, but was now living in Washington, DC. Her children were all grown and had their homes. As for my father, well, he was still living in the old house in Woodbridge, the same house that was built with the help of Mr. Tyrrell. When I did come down from New York to DC, I would stay with my sister for a few days and then visit my father in Woodbridge.

On one of my visits to my father, I remember seeing Bud Cigar, whose last name was "Weeks." However, everyone called him Bud Cigar. He was an elderly White man who was a close friend of my father. When I arrived at my father's house, Bud Cigar was sitting in an old beaten-up car, which I believed was a Packard, parked in the front yard. The doors were wide open. Inside the car were rags, empty beer cans, and lots of trash. The whole scene was awful to look at and very disgusting. One would think it was a landfill for dumping trash. Bud Cigar was playing with an ugly old dog, which was on a lease, thank God. Shack, my father, was asleep in the house. I went inside, woke him up, and stayed with him and his buddy Bud Cigar for a few hours. Shack and Bud Cigar were drinking partners. They loved sitting around drinking beer, wine, and liquor. They didn't bother anyone. Shack would smoke his Pall Malls or Camel cigarettes, and Bud Cigar would smoke his cigars.

# BEYOND KANKEY HILL

Shack's place with torn couch and old wood stove.

Shack's bed and trash all over.

After sitting and chatting with Shack and Bud Cigar for a few hours, it was time for me to leave and go back to DC to my sister's apartment and get ready to travel back to New York.

Then there was another time, I believe the year was 1968, when I traveled down from New York to DC and Virginia to visit my sister and my father. When I got to my father's house, my brother Puddin was in the front yard. He told me he just ran Bud Cigar off the property and for him not to come back. I asked Puddin what happened. His reply was that every time he comes by to see our father, Bud Cigar and Shack would be sitting around half drunk and drinking. I personally didn't see anything wrong with it. Shack and Bud Cigar were just two old good friends, like the two men in the movie *I'm Not Rappaport* starring late Walter Matthau and Ossie Davis. One happened to be White and the other Black.

My father always kept beer or wine stored away somewhere on the property. He occasionally had a bottle of liquor hidden somewhere too. Because he didn't have a refrigerator, he usually kept the beer and wine buried under some leaves or bushes in the back yard. That way, the beer and wine would stay cool. Whenever his friends would come by, be they Black or White, my father would go outside, look under the leaves or bushes, and pull out a few cans of beer or a bottle of wine. If they were drinking whiskey or wine, my dad would take a swig and pass the bottle around. Everyone drank out of the same bottle. Besides being an honest, hard-working, good Black man, Shack was admired by many people. When he died in August of 1971, just as many Whites were at his funeral as there were Blacks.

## BEYOND KANKEY HILL

After all my trips between New York, DC, and Virginia, I always went back to work at the FRBNY. One summer after I got off work from the bank, I taught a class in stage acting to young teenagers in Bronx, New York. The city's mayor, John Lindsay, in 1970 had created a Summer Program Project to help inspire Youths of the City. I got in touch with the mayor's office and stated that I would like to work with that Summer Program Project. There was a job opening for someone to work with kids in the Bronx. The job wouldn't be paying much, and it was only to be one day a week, 6 p.m. to 8 p.m., for seven weeks. I took the job.

After I got off work from the bank, I would take the Lexington Avenue subway going uptown to the Grand Concourse in the Bronx. Once there, I went into the community room of the building in that area and started teaching the teenagers. I believe there were twelve or fifteen of them. The first day, I could see I was going to have a problem with these teenagers. What happened was I was about ten minutes in the classroom teaching my students when three big bully-looking teenage boys came inside and started laughing, giggling, and acting up. Even though they were way bigger than me, even bigger than the students in my classroom, I wasn't scared. In fact, I was very polite. I said to them, "Hey guys. I bet you can't do that again." They looked at me and said, "Do what?" I told the three of them to go back out in the hallway, to come back in, and to *act* the same way, and say the same words they did when they first came in my classroom. They did. They went back out in the hallway and came back in the classroom. Then I told them to do the same movements, repeat the same words, and show the same facial expressions as they did on their very first entrance.

Oh, they were quite surprised when I told them what they left out. I told them about the difference between their actions from the first entrance to the second entrance. On their second entrance, I let those boys know that their facial expressions were different, their walk was different, and their talk was different. Nearly everything they did on that second entrance was different from what they did and said on their first entrance when they interrupted my class. After I told them what they did and didn't do, they got interested in the classwork. They started asking questions about acting, movies, television, and so on.

The second week I went back to teach the class, those same three boys were right there in the classroom. They didn't miss one class out of the seven weeks during my teaching. They got along very well with the other students. The whole incident was like a family reunion. A bunch of kids coming together and getting along. My last day of teaching was a little emotional. All the kids gathered around me, hugged me, and thanked me. They wanted me to stay for the rest of the summer. I told them the city's program was only for seven weeks. Those kids told me that they needed something like the acting class they had taken with me. They felt that taking that class gave them something to do in the evenings, instead of hanging out in the streets. The more I think of those kids now, I get reflections of the actor Sidney Poitier in the movie *To Sir with Love*. The movie shows Mr. Poitier portraying a high school teacher to some disorderly kids in London. For me, I believe all kids need attention. They need someone they can talk to, relate to, and is willing to listen to them. Most of all, they need mentors. Now I am no psychologist or sociologist, but I strongly believe kids have more goodness in them than badness.

## BEYOND KANKEY HILL

After finishing the summer job with the youths in the Bronx, it was business as usual—work, going to the theatre, shopping, dining out, classes, and keeping politically active. I remember during the 1960s and the 1970s, I became very conscientious about race and injustice in this country. On my job at the Federal Reserve Bank, guys started calling me "Rap." They were comparing me to H. Rap Brown, the Black civil rights activist and member of the Black Panther Party. I would often come to work dressed in a suit and I would wear a black beret, which was similar to the one the Black Panthers wore. Although I was not a member of that party, and had no intention of joining it, I did believe in the group's idea of clothing, educating, and feeding the hungry children in deprived neighborhoods. I went along with that idea. I thought it was great.

I remember one evening, when I had just gotten off from working at the Federal Reserve Bank, I took the 20-minute subway ride from downtown Manhattan to uptown 6$^{th}$ Avenue and Greenwich Street. At the corner of Greenwich Street, where it meets 6$^{th}$ Avenue, I stood and passed out flyers for the Black Panthers "End the Hunger" program. It was during the same time Angela Davis, another civil rights activist, was jailed at the Women's Detention House located at the same location. As I was passing out the flyers, I noticed a group of protesters shouting "Free Angela Davis, Free Angela Davis" in front of the Women's Detention House. I, too, joined the protesters who wanted Angela Davis freed. The detention house was a big, old, tall, red brick building. We didn't know what floor Angela was on. We just looked up and kept shouting "Free Angela Davis, Free Angela Davis." Someone in the crowd, which was quite diverse, gave me a small round lapel button showing the face of Angela that read "Free Angela Davis."

Often times when I went to work, I would wear the button on my shirt or suit jacket. Some White people, when they saw the button, they would give me a funny look and turn their heads. I think they were more afraid of the button than me. White folks really got upset whenever I wore a dashiki or a kufi cap to work. I believe they felt intimidated. Then there were some Blacks who didn't like the way I dressed either. Those Blacks were considered the Uncle Toms and Aunt Janes of that time, meaning they were representing signs of slavery.

Years later, 1988 to 1991, I served as the President of the NAACP Greenwich Village Branch in Manhattan. After serving as president for three years, I decided to step down. One must remember, I was still working a 9 to 5 job. I just wouldn't be able to go to every annual NAACP convention, which most times were held somewhere else other than in New York. However, relinquishing my position as president didn't stop me from staying active in civil rights issues. Overtly, New York's Blacks were suffering a tremendous amount of social injustice.

On December 20, 1986, a mob of White youths chased Michael Griffith, a Black man, onto the Belt Parkway in Howard Beach, Queens, NY. While running away from the mob, Griffith was hit and killed on the parkway. In Bensonhurst, Queens, August of 1989, a mob of White boys killed Yusef Hawkins, who was only sixteen and Black. Bensonhurst was a White neighborhood and Blacks were not wanted there. On August 9, 1997, a Brooklyn Haitian man by the name of Abner Louima was beaten and brutally harmed by rough cops, who broke off a broomstick and sexually assaulted Louima. The assault shocked many people, including some Whites. When the trial came up, there were some days when I was able to sit in the Brooklyn courthouse and listen to the hearings. Then there was the Amadou Diallo case in February of 1999. White Cops killed Diallo when they thought the wallet that he was carrying was a gun. At the trial, all the cops were found not guilty. People in New York were outraged. They were fed up with the senseless acts and killings of innocent Black folks. It seemed like *Black lives didn't matter*. Black people were tired of being mistreated. They weren't going to take it anymore. There were protest marches and more protest marches. Yes, I was in many of them, along with the Rev. Al Sharpton and other civil rights activists. In one of the marches, I remember greeting the author, activist, professor, and doctor Cornell West. We, the marchers, had just crossed over the Brooklyn Bridge and were near Chambers Street in lower Manhattan. I ran up to Dr. West and said, "Dr. West, you are our hero. You are *our* Albert Einstein." He turned to me, grabbed my hand, and said, "Thank you my brother, thank you." Dr. West has many titles in front of his name. But the title I give him is the title of "genius." The man is absolutely brilliant. I say that with no hesitation.

 In the early 1980s, during the month of January, I traveled from New York to Washington, DC, many times, desiring to help make Martin Luther King, Jr.'s birthday a national holiday. Me and hundreds of other participants marched down Pennsylvania Avenue over to the Lincoln Memorial. On one occasion, I remember standing on a block of ice in freezing weather in front of the Memorial, listening to various speakers calling for Congress to make Dr. King's birthday a national holiday. I was so cold. But I felt, as a man of color, it was my obligation to participate in these well-planned endeavors. Finally, after years of marches and speeches, we the people got our request answered. In November of 1983, President Ronald Reagan signed the congressional bill making Martin Luther King, Jr.'s birthday a national holiday.

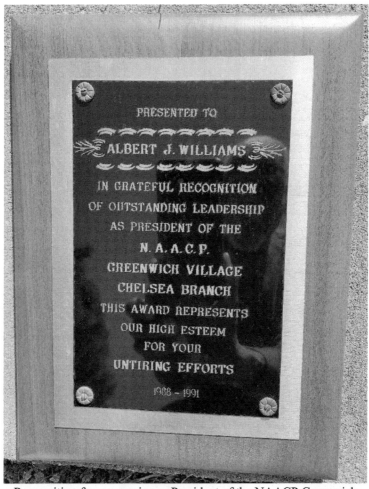

Recognition for my service as President of the NAACP Greenwich Village Chelsea Branch in New York City.

## CHAPTER 6
## Trips to Europe

No matter how busy I was in New York, I always found time to take a vacation. I remember I made my first trip to Europe in the mid-1970s. I was still working at the Federal Reserve Bank of New York in the financial district of Manhattan.

One day when I went to lunch, a guy on Broadway and Chamber's Street approached me and asked me some questions about Manhattan. He asked me something like, "How do I get to Times Square? Is it in walking distance?" I told him how to get there and that it was not far. He then asked me if I could hold some money for him because, according to him, he was scheduled to meet some woman at this corner of Broadway and Chambers Street and didn't want to have a lot of money on him when he met the woman. Next, he showed me a brown paper bag with a big roll of money in it and asked if I could hold it for him and come back in an hour at this same location. I told him that I was on my lunch hour and may not be able to get away from my job. He kept insisting and again showed me that bag of money. He asked me where do I keep my money. I told him that I keep my money in my pocket. He says to me, "Put your money in this bag with my money and hold on to it." So, I did. He gave me the bag and said to me, "Now, make sure you're back here in an hour." I said, "Okay," and I went back to work.

When I got back to my job, a few of my fellow co-workers and I went to the locker room, where we often took a break from the job. I said to the guys, "Fellers, look, I got a bag of money. This guy on Broadway gave me all this money to hold for him." I emptied the brown paper bag out on the table. I was stunned! Absolutely stunned! Only thing in the bag was a bunch of napkins. Yes, napkins!!! He had switched brown paper bags on me and I didn't even notice. The guys just laughed at me. Yes, I was robbed. I had put close to five hundred dollars in that brown bag, which I thought contained money. I don't know what I was thinking at the time. Foolish, foolish me. The incident happened on a Friday, the day before I was to leave for Europe. But you know what I did after I got off work? I went straight to First National City Bank, made a withdrawal, went to the American Express Building, got traveler checks, and headed home. On my way home, I stopped at the downtown Manhattan Police Station and told the officers what had happened to me. They looked at me as if I was crazy. They said, "Sir, you fell for a con game. It's called a Murphy." I thought to myself how stupid I was not to have known it was a con game. Things happen in life.

The next day, Saturday, I was on a KLM flight out of JFK heading to Europe. I had to change flights in Iceland. It was only a short layover, maybe one or two hours. I then boarded the TWA flight to Brussels. Once in Brussels, I took the train up to Amsterdam and then down to Luxembourg. I remember when the train stopped in Antwerp, Belgium, a young boy and girl got on board. They both had back sacks. The boy asked me if I was from America, and I said, "Yes." He then went on and asked me if America was really like *Midnight Cowboy*. I didn't really know what to say, because I had never seen the movie.

I tell anyone, if you really want to see Europe, take the train (often called The Rail). I saw some of the most awesome sights in the world traveling via train through Europe. Riding through the mountains and seeing the Alps was breathtaking. Not only does Europe have great sceneries, but everywhere I went people treated me quite well. I was really surprised when I got to Munich, Germany. Whenever I asked for directions or what attractions I should visit, the Germans always made sure that I understood what they were saying. At times, they would even draw a map of the directions for me. I couldn't speak German, other than the words "danke sehr," which means "Thank you very much." When I went to Amsterdam, it was a must that I visit Anne Frank's family house. I felt sad as I toured that house on this first trip to Amsterdam. It's the house where a little Jewish girl and her family had to hide in the attic from the Nazis during World War II. The house is now a museum. Years later when I went back to Amsterdam, I visited that same house and felt sad all over again.

Amsterdam has an area known as "The Red-Light District." I had heard about the district and seen stories on American television about the area. One afternoon, while sightseeing and strolling through the streets of Amsterdam, I came upon a little alley, which I decided to walk down. I did not know that this little alley was the Red-Light District. Lo and behold, I saw some of the most beautiful-looking women in the world standing in door fronts and display windows. I've never seen nothing like it. The men walking through the alley were being propositioned to come into the women's quarters. As I was walking through the alley of prostitutes (yes, that's what they were, prostitutes, the oldest profession in the world, some say), one of them reached out so close to me until she almost touched me. It was shocking to see prostitutes soliciting so openly. Then again, prostitution was legal in Amsterdam. No, I did not surrender to their invitation. I left that area saying to myself, "Wow, unbelievable."

The hotel I stayed in was the Victoria Damrak 1-5, located at N1 1012 Lg Amsterdam, Netherlands, and was in walking distance from the train station called Grand Central Station. Nearby, there was a little café called "Harlem." I remember going inside and ordering a brew. On the wall were pictures of jazz musicians and pictures of the Harlem Renaissance era of the 1920s and 1930s.

After spending four or five days in Amsterdam, it was now time to go to Paris, France. The train ride from Amsterdam to Paris took longer than I thought it would. I don't know exactly how long it took, but to me, it was quite long. Maybe two or three hours. While in Paris, I stayed in a hotel on the Right Bank. You see, Paris is divided into two sections. One section is known as the Left Bank and the other is known as the Right Bank. The Left Bank is mostly tourists, whereas the Right Bank is mostly the real Parisians. The Seine River separates the two banks.

On one of my many trips to France, I remember sitting next to a young lady on her way to study at Sorbonne Université, which is on the Left Bank in Paris. When I met her, I said to myself, "It must be nice to study abroad."

While in Paris, I visited many art galleries and museums, but my favorite museum was the Louvre. It was there that I saw the original painting of the *Mona Lisa* by Leonardo da Vinci. I was surprised that the picture was so small in size. Anyone visiting Paris must visit the Louvre and view some of greatest paintings in the world. But you must be prepared to deal with the long lines and the crowd.

Me in the lobby at the Louvre.

I was in awe when I walked down the street known as Avenue des Champs-Élysées, which starts at the Arc de Triomphe. I wonder how did the late Josephine Baker, the world's renowned entertainer, feel when she walked down that famous avenue. The avenue contains buildings that are truly a tour de force in their architectural design. Everywhere I looked were expensive stores, such as Cartier and Louis Vuitton. Right off the avenue was a mall called Galeries Lafayette Paris. Inside you could find purveyors of high-quality merchandise. It's my favorite mall in all the world. Yes, *Paris, Mon Amour.*

Me in Paris in front of the Eiffel Tower.

When I arrived in Paris, people treated me very well there too. They welcomed me and even helped me with my broken French. I felt comfortable. I now understand why so many Blacks went and lived in France in the 1930s and 40s. Prominent Blacks, such as Nobel Peace Prize winner

Ralph Bunche, and entertainers like Eartha Kitt, Nina Simone, Josephine Baker, and even the great famous writer James Baldwin lived there.

During another trip to Europe, which occurred in the mid-1980s, I visited some of the same places I did on my previous trips. One thing different was I learned how to travel via the Metro. So, one day I decided to venture outside of Paris. I took the Metro south to Versailles to see the Château de Versailles and all of its grandeur gardens. Touring Versailles was wonderful. Truly an amazing site. One could spend all day there and still not see everything.

Me in Versailles.

The next day, after visiting Versailles, I decided to take a train ride down to Nice, pronounced like the English noun "niece." It is located in the region called Côte d'Azur, and is the capital of the French Riviera. The train passed through Cannes, France (known as the film festival capital of the world), and finally arrived in Nice. I got off the train, put my luggage in a locker at the station, and boarded a small country bus for a ride to Monaco.

The bus ride wasn't bad. As a matter of fact, the ride was quite lovely and very enchanting. As I looked out the window, I saw the beautiful Mediterranean Sea on my right side and great-looking, mountainous landscape rocks and greenery on my left side. The bus traveled over roads that were extremely narrow and twisting. The ride did become a little scary at times because the driver appeared to be driving right alongside the edge of the rocky cliff's terrain. Nevertheless, I was still excited. Continuing to look out the window, I was able to see through the wooded hills where former American actress Princess Grace Kelly and her husband Prince Rainier III of Monaco lived. The whole area was beautifully laid out with huge trees, gorgeous homes, and cultivated greenery.

When I got off the bus in Monaco, I walked around the area for a while. Then I went swimming in the Mediterranean Sea. The water was crystal clear. I didn't see much sand on the beach. Mostly what I saw were various colored pebbles covering the sand. The pebbles looked so beautiful and magnificent, I just had to bring some back with me to the USA. From where I was in Monaco, I could see Casino de Monte-Carlo, the place where the rich and famous go. I wasn't famous, and I certainly wasn't rich. When I asked a local Frenchman how to get there, he told me how and that I needed to have a suit and tie on in order to go inside the casino. Oh well, I didn't have a suit and tie with me, so the trip to Casino de Monte-Carlo was out. No matter what, I still enjoyed my short stay in Monaco and that part of the French territory.

The next day I was on the train again. This time I headed to Rome, Italy. When I arrived at the train station in Rome, I was quickly approached by a gypsy woman who had a small child in her arms. The woman was begging for money. I believe I gave her a few Liras. At the time, Liras were the money being used in Italy. I had used Marks in Germany and French Francs in France. You see, whenever I arrived in any of those countries, I would always go to a money exchange outlet and have some of my American money exchanged for the type of money being used in the appropriate country. It was a little confusing at times, but I had my little notebook showing me the value of each piece of coin/currency. Today, Germany, France, and Italy use what is called the "Euro," which came into existence in 2002.

In Rome, I visited the Vatican, the Colosseum, various flea markets, and the gravesite where Julius Caesar is said to be buried. Some of the best pizza I've ever had was in Rome. All in all, I had a great time on this trip.

The last time I went to Europe was in August of 2009. I boarded a 13-hour nonstop United Airlines flight out of Dulles International Airport in Chantilly, Virginia, to Charles de Gaulle Airport in Paris, France. Once I arrived in France, I took a taxi to the hotel where I would be staying. The hotel was the Best Western Montcalm Hotel located at 50 Avenue, Félix Faure, 75015 Paris, France. After settling down in my room, I decided to write a little in my memoir journal. When I got ready to go to bed, I turned on the TV and there was breaking news that Senator Ted Kennedy had died. My heart dropped. I said to myself, "Wow, another Kennedy gone." I was somewhat depressed and very sad, because I liked Mr. Kennedy. I got off the bed, got dressed, and went out and just walked and walked all over Paris. Yes, it was nighttime. But I wasn't afraid. Anyone who's been to Paris knows that it is a beautiful city at night too. After walking around about three or four hours, I went back to my hotel and went to sleep. I spent six nights in Paris.

Then I went to Brussels, yes, via train. In Brussels, I stayed at a four-star hotel called Eurostars Grand Place Hotel located at Boulevard Anspach, 1000 Brussels, Belgium. It was a fabulous hotel with all its grandeur and splendor. Great buffet and wonderful service. Shopping was close by too. When you walked down the streets, on either side, you would see perfectly manicured flower gardens. Actually, I felt like I was in a florist shop. After spending one night and one day in Brussels, I took the train ride from Brussels to Amsterdam. It was a two-hour train ride, stopping along the way to pick up other passengers. I was enjoying every bit of the ride. It gave me time to see other beautiful landscapes of Europe. On this trip, I only spent two nights in Amsterdam. No, I didn't visit the "Red-Light District" on this trip. But I did a lot of shopping for clothes. I especially bought some shirts, which were all imported to Amsterdam from Italy. After six nights in Paris, one night in Brussels, and two nights in Amsterdam, my time in Europe was up. I caught a United Airlines flight out of Schiphol Airport, Amsterdam, Netherlands, nonstop to Dulles International Airport. In no time, I was back home in the Good Old USA.

Shopping at the Académie Nationale de Musique, Paris, France.

# ALBERT J. WILLIAMS

On a boat on the Seine River, Paris, France.

# CHAPTER 7
# Show Business

Across from my apartment on Bank Street was a theatrical school called HB Studio, and it offered courses in Playwriting and Acting. The studio was managed by Herbert Berghof and his wife, Uta Hagen. The two of them, along with other staff teachers, taught those courses to any student who wanted to learn how to write plays and act in television, movies, and on the stage. Because the school was right in front of my apartment, and I had always wanted to be an actor, I decided to take a course in acting at the school. I studied directly under the instruction of Mr. Berghof, and I had to read, study, and perform scenes from various play scripts. Studying under the direction of Mr. Berghof, I learned quite a bit about theatrical acting. I learned the various stage positions for acting on the stage, how to control the voice, and how to make a character believable. Former students of the HB Studio included Robert De Niro, Joy Behar, Debbie Allen, Anne Bancroft, Whoopie Goldberg, and many other well-known artists. Sometimes when I walked through the neighborhood, I would see Mr. Berghof out walking his dog. I never met Ms. Hagen, but I did know she had won a Broadway Tony Award for best actress in the play called *Who's Afraid of Virginia Woolf?*

HB studio was not the only acting school I attended. For a very short period, I attended the New York Academy of Theatrical Arts, which I believe was located on 5$^{th}$

Avenue in Manhattan. While there, I studied under the direction of the late Philip Nolan.

After leaving that school, I enrolled in the Senior Dramatic Workshop at Carnegie Hall on West $57^{th}$ Street in Midtown Manhattan. The workshop had formerly been known as The New Dramatist, and was under the direction of Erwin Piscator, a well-known German playwright, actor, and poet. After his death, the school took on a new name, Senior Dramatic Workshop, and was headed by Saul Colin. As a student of Mr. Colin, I remember two statements he made, which have stayed with me all through my acting career. The first one was, "No one can teach you how to act, only the techniques of acting." The second one was, "Good stage actors usually make good film actors, but good film actors don't always make good stage actors." I believe both statements are true, because if you master the techniques for the stage, you can use those techniques when working in movies and television. When Mr. Colin cast and directed me in Edna St. Vincent Millay's play *Aria da Capo*, I used some of the acting techniques I had learned in his class in creating the character of Thyrsis. Many well-known actors had gone to this acting school at Carnegie Hall, including Marlon Brando, Tony Curtis, Harry Belafonte, Shelley Winters, to name a few. I must say, I always learned something from all of the acting schools I attended. I don't regret going to any of them.

New York had two publications, *Back Stage* and *Show Business*, that were published once a week. Each publication would list open casting calls and production companies that were seeking actors for various shows. I picked up those publications every week and started going to casting calls and auditions. The very first casting call I went to was in 1970 for a movie called *Cotton Comes to Harlem*, starring the comedian Redd Foxx. The movie was to be filmed in Harlem, and the production company was seeking background actors (also known as extras) for the film. When I went to the casting call, there were over two hundred people waiting in line to be interviewed by the casting director. I was cast as a background player, portraying a chef.

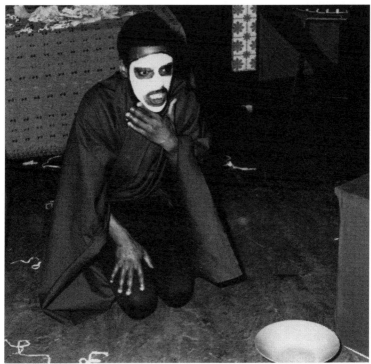

Me in Edna St. Vincent Millay's play *Aria da Capo*.

The wardrobe designer fitted me in a chef's outfit for one scene, and the next day I wore regular clothes in a crowd scene. The entire film was shot in Harlem. When I went to the theatre to see the film, all I saw was the back of my head covered with a chef's hat. But it was a good experience working with other actors. Redd Foxx was just as funny off stage as he was on stage. One day, the director, Mr. Ossie Davis, gave the crew and all the actors a one-hour lunch break. Redd Foxx went to his limousine and the back door was open. The temperature that day had to be over 100 degrees. A laughing crowd had gathered around Mr. Foxx, and I wanted to see what all the laughing was about. When I got near the crowd, there was Mr. Foxx with his shirt off, sitting on the back seat of the limousine. He was showing everyone his nipple, which had the drawing of a face and eyes around it. The nipple represented the nose, and Mr. Foxx made the muscles in his nipple wiggle. I cracked up laughing, as did everyone else. The whole scene was quite hilarious.

After working on that film, I decided to get a professional photographer to take some pictures of me so I could mail them out to different casting directors and agencies. Once the photos were made, I sent them, along with my resume, to nearly every casting agent and advertising agency in New York City. I even sent my photo/resume to the three major networks—NBC, ABC, and CBS—with hope of landing an acting job. I started getting jobs in a few off-Broadway plays, like *You Can't Take It with You*, *Big Time Buck White*, *The Billie Holiday Story*, *The Dutchman,* and a few other plays. I was constantly sending out my photos/resumes.

It wasn't long after sending them out that I started getting calls to work as an extra on different movies. Even the casting directors at the three major TV networks started calling me and casting me as an extra. The pay was good because I was a member of the unions called SAG/AFTRA (Screen Actors Guild and American Federation of Television and Radio Artists), and I had to be paid union-scale pay. All the soap operas I appeared in were filmed in New York. Just to name a few of those soaps, there was *The Guiding Light* (which I appeared on for nearly 17 years, under a non-contract), *One Life to Live*, *All My Children* (nearly five years), *Ryan's Hope, The Doctors,* and *Search for Tomorrow.* I enjoyed working on the soaps and other TV shows because it gave me the knowledge of how important camera angles are in shooting a scene. Most of the time, there would be a camera A, a camera B, and a camera C. All the cameras would shoot a scene from different angles.

Me on *The Guiding Light.*

In 1990, I had a recurring role for a whole season as the newspaper vendor on *The Cosby Show.* The show was filmed every week at the Astoria Studios in Queens, New York. Other television shows I've worked on include *New York Undercover, Law & Order, The Wire,* and a PBS show called *Between the Lions.* Movies I've worked on include the following: *The Associate* (starring Whoppi

Goldberg), *Sweet and Lowdown* (starring Sean Penn), *Coming to America* (starring Eddie Murphy), *Lincoln* (starring Daniel Day-Lewis) and *Heartburn* (starring Meryl Streep and Jack Nicholson). Besides the films I've mentioned, I know I've worked on at least 80 or more films.

Some of the movies and television shows I've worked on bring back fond memories. Besides the funniness of Redd Foxx in *Cotton Comes to Harlem*, there was the funniness of Eddie Murphy in *Coming to America*, filmed in 1988. On the latter film and towards its beginning, there's a scene where me and a young kid playing my son are sitting at a table, and we are pretending to be eating breakfast. Mr. Murphy's character comes in and looks at me and the kid eating. While cleaning and mopping around the table, Mr. Murphy starts a dialogue with me saying something like, "Oh, I see you got good sense. You're eating McNuggets." I say to him, "Get away from us man. Can't you see we're eating?" The whole scene takes place just before Samuel Jackson's character comes in and shoots up the restaurant. When I went to the theatre to see the movie, I saw myself and the kid sitting at the table, but my dialogue was edited out. I was a little disappointed.

In 1986, I was cast as a background player on the movie *Heartburn,* a romantic comedy starring Meryl Streep and Jack Nicholson. When the director, Mike Nichols, gave everyone on the set a fifteen-minute break, Meryl Streep came over to me and said, "Hello, I'm Meryl. Is everyone treating you all right on the set?" I said, "Oh yes, everything is fine." I was in awe. MERYL STREEP? Taking time out of her busy schedule to see if I was all right? Wow! I was very much impressed with her kindness. When I went to the theatre to see the film, I did see a close-up shot of me dressed in a tuxedo sitting at a dinner table.

Another time I wore a tuxedo in a film was when I worked on a movie called *The Associate,* starring Whoppie Goldberg. Ms. Goldberg tried to get me upgraded from a background player to a bit part. Bit parts are parts in a script that call for an actor to perform a special task. Plus, the pay is higher. I played a cigar man passing out cigars. Whoopie put in her character's dialogue, something like, "You see that man passing out cigars? He could be up here on this stage doing the same thing I'm doing." When she said that, of course, the cameraman had to put the camera on me passing out cigars because Whoppie's character had pointed to me as the cigar man. The director, Daniel Petrie, took me to the side and told me what to do while passing out the cigars. In the scene, all the men, including actor Eli Wallach, are dressed in tuxedos. The character that Whoppie was portraying makes a speech, and at the end of the speech I start the scene off by slowly clapping my hands, which incites the other actors to slowly join in the clapping, which eventually turns into a loud applause. When I went to the theatre to see the film, there I was on the big movie screen again.

As for working on movies, I think my biggest joy and my biggest disappointment was in 2012, when I landed a speaking part in Steven Spielberg's movie *Lincoln,* starring Daniel Day-Lewis. I was cast as a contraband (similar to a preacher). I was so excited. I told my church members, my friends, and my family. I was spreading the news of my good fortune, being cast in a Spielberg movie. The scene was shot late one night in Richmond, Virginia. I had learned my lines and almost knew them backwards. I put my heart and soul in the character I portrayed. The scene called for me to interact with Mr. Lincoln and speak directly to him as he passed through a crowd of slaves. After rehearsing the scene one or two times, Mr. Spielberg came over to me, introduced himself, and gave me a few specifics. When the scene was finally taped, he called for everyone's attention. There must have been at least 50 to 70 some extras in the scene. Mr. Spielberg said, "The Oscar goes to Albert." I believe he was just being kind when he said that. But my joy disappeared when I went to the theatre to see the film. The whole scene with the slaves and me had been edited out. I don't know if it was because the scene was shot at night and the lighting was bad, or edited out because of the length of the film, which runs for two hours and thirty minutes. That's show business for you. When you do a film, you don't know if you're going to end up on the screen or on the cutting room floor.

My audition photo for *Lincoln*.

## BEYOND KANKEY HILL

My work on television shows had its memorable moments too. Take the daytime soap called *The Guiding Light*, which I appeared on for nearly 17 years. In one of the episodes, I portrayed a jazz musician who was a horn player. Before shooting the scene, I was practicing holding the horn one day when one of the male principal actors came over to me and asked if I knew how to play the horn. I told him I didn't. Then he asked to see the horn, and I gave it to him. He went on and showed me how the horn should be held and where to place my fingers. He did a good demonstration. The next day when I went to the studio to continue working on the show, he saw me again and smilingly asked me if I now knew how to hold that horn. I smiled and told him, "I think so." A few minutes later, some of the other extras approached me and asked me if I knew who that was that showed me how to hold the horn. I told them I didn't. Come to find out, he was Elizabeth Taylor's son Michael Wilding Jr. The next time I saw him on the set, I paid more attention to him. I noticed that his eyes were a bluest violet color, and his hair was jet black, just like his mother's. He was a very friendly guy. Always spoke. He would say, "Good morning" or "How's it going?" Just a regular down-to-earth person. I remember one afternoon seeing his mother, Elizabeth Taylor, in front of Macy's on 34$^{th}$ Street in Manhattan. She was there promoting her perfume Black Diamond for women, and her cologne Passion for men. She was rather short in stature, but gorgeous. She even had a little dog with her.

Another daytime soap, called *All My Children*, had its memorable moments too. I worked four years on that show when it was being filmed in New York and before it moved to California. One day I had to be at the ABC studio at 7 a.m. After wardrobe check, and hair and makeup, all the extras were to act like passengers at a make-believe airport. We finished shooting the scene very early that day. Must had been around 11 a.m. As I was about to exit the building, so was Susan Lucci. On her way to the limousine waiting outside for her, she turns to me and says, "Isn't it nice getting out early?" I said, "Yes, it is." I thought to myself, it must be nice to have a limo waiting to take you home. I walked to the subway station and took the downtown train home.

On the daytime soap *One Life to Live*, I did get to speak in one episode of the show. I had what's known as U/5, which means the actor will have five lines or less. The scene took place in a boardroom setting and called on the characters to vote on a situation. When it came to my character, Judge Morris, I was asked by one of the main actors how do I vote. I said one word, "No." When that episode aired on TV, I did see myself as I uttered that one word, "No." Even though I've never portrayed a major character in a movie or television show, I loved working on them. One of my acting teachers, Dr. Edwin Colin, once told me, "There are no small roles, only small actors."

My sister loved seeing me on the soaps. She had retired from Fort Belvoir and was living in Washington, DC. The retirement allowed her more time to watch all her favorite daytime soap operas. She would even call me in New York and ask me what was going to happen to certain characters on a show. I told her I didn't know because I *really* didn't know.

Although Sis was living in DC, she maintained a parcel of land totaling one acre in Woodbridge. The land was given to her by our dad, Shack. He had already given me a parcel of about 1.3 acres in 1963, a few months just before I went into the Army. The two parcels of land were adjacent to each other. Sis didn't want to live in DC any longer and wanted to move back to Virginia so she could be closer to her grandchildren. She decided to list her parcel of land with a realtor called Red Carpet, whose office was on Rte. 1 in Woodbridge. The realtor put a "For Sale" sign in the front yard of the old cinder block house, which was the same house made from the material Harry Tyrrell had given Shack. That realty sign stayed in the front yard well over five years. The realtor was having trouble trying to find someone to buy the property, and Sis was constantly telling me how she just wanted to sell it and get out of DC.

After finding out she was tired of living in DC, and I didn't like the idea of her being unhappy, I asked her if she would sell it to me if I paid her what she was asking. She wanted to know what would I do with it. I told her I would have that old cinder block house torn down and put a new house in its place. I went on to tell her that she could live in the new house and I would make the monthly mortgage payments and pay the property taxes. All she had to do was pay the monthly utilities bills. She was excited about the idea. So, I went ahead and paid her what she wanted for the property, which was the same amount listed with the realtor. After all the legal work was done, I had the two parcels (her parcel and my parcel) joined.

In December of 1988, I started looking at sellers of modular homes in Virginia. I looked in Stafford and Fredericksburg, Virginia. Finally, I found a seller in Alexandria and I liked the modular homes that were on display. I ended up buying one called The Mansion, which was almost 28 feet x 60 feet (1680 square feet). One thing about modular homes, if you contact the manufacturer before the modular is completely built, you can practically customize it the way you want it built. I did that and was very pleased with the outcome. After all the excavating and obtaining permits from the county, the modular was finally put on the property in September of 1989. I furnished most of the house with brand-new furniture.

A few months later, November to be exact, Sis left Washington and moved to the new home a week before Thanksgiving. I still had my apartment in New York, which kept me going back and forth from there to Virginia. As for my acting career, I was getting a lot of calls to work on the soaps and movies. Show business had picked up and was working in my favor. Seems like every week I was hitting the streets of Manhattan, auditioning here, auditioning there, going on casting calls, interviews, on and on. If anyone deserves an Oscar or TV Emmy for most appearances in background work, it certainly should be me. It was a great time in my life, a life I think I wouldn't have had if I hadn't moved beyond Kankey Hill.

Years later, around 1997 or 1998, Sis started telling me she felt the house was way too big for one person. Frankly speaking, I didn't know what to do. I've always wanted Sis to be happy. I wanted her to get whatever she desired. She was the mother I never had. I remember whenever I would come down from New York to see her, she always appeared happy to see me. However, sadness would come whenever I got ready to leave Virginia and head back to New York. As I drove out of the driveway, Sis would be standing and waving at me from the front door and I'd be waving back at her. I'd be teary-eyed all the way up Interstate 95 to the New Jersey Turnpike heading to New York.

# BEYOND KANKEY HILL

On October 4, 1999, Sis was hospitalized at the Potomac Hospital in Woodbridge. The next day, October 5, I was on a Greyhound bus out of New York heading to Woodbridge. I had to see my motherly, beloved sister. She had surgery on October 11 and was in and out of the hospital until 2002. On July 5, 2002, I woke that morning around 7 a.m. because I knew I had to take my sister to the hospital for her medical treatment. When I left my bedroom and started back to my sister's room, there she was with the oxygen hose hanging from her nose, lying on the floor. I kept calling her. She wasn't breathing. She had no pulse. I said to myself, "This can't be. No, this just can't be, please." I called downstairs and summoned her visiting granddaughter to come upstairs. When she got upstairs and saw her grandmother lying on the floor, she became hysterical. I called the police. My motherly, beloved Sis died July 5, 2002.

My brother Puddin and my sister Doris (Sis).

# ALBERT J. WILLIAMS

Dressed for my part in Woody Allen's *Sweet and Lowdown*, 1998.

On the set of the *John Adams* mini-series in 2008.

# ALBERT J. WILLIAMS

On the set of the *John Adams* mini-series in 2008.

Ossie Davis and me on the set of *I'm Not Rappaport*.

In my dressing room for *The Guiding Light*.

In my dressing room for *The Guiding Light*.

Me (second) in *Primary Colors* with John Travolta.

On the set of the *John Adams* mini-series in 2008.

# BEYOND KANKEY HILL

Head and body shots sent out to producers/casting directors.

# ALBERT J. WILLIAMS

**Albert Williams**
SAG / AFTRA

# BEYOND KANKEY HILL

The Doctor

The Mean Judge

The Casual Look

The Fisherman

Height: 5'7" • Weight: 135 • Eyes: Brown • Hair: Gray
Shoe: 9 • Suit Size: 36S • Waist: 29 • Inseam: 30

# ALBERT J. WILLIAMS

Me at my last New York City apartment, 379 West Street.

# CHAPTER 8
# Moving Back to Virginia

After my sister died, I was in a quandary. I had to make a decision to either keep my nice comfortable apartment in New York and rent my house out in Virginia, or move back there. I chose the latter. So, in November of 2002, four months after my sister's passing, I vacated my apartment in New York and moved to my house in Woodbridge, which wasn't as segregated as it was when I left in the 1960s. It was now a little more diverse. But I must say, during my youth when I was growing up here in Woodbridge, it was very much segregated, especially most of Prince William County. At the time, there was very little shopping available. Plus, the communities didn't have much industry or opportunities for Colored folks. As the county started to change in the 1960s with the building of Dale City, so did the infrastructure of the county. There was the construction of Marumsco Plaza (which wasn't all that pleasant to Colored folks), and in the 1980s, the Potomac Mills Shopping Center.

Although I miss the ambiance of New York, I have gradually adjusted to life in Virginia. I don't regret moving back to Woodbridge. The move allows me to enjoy planting vegetables every year, do yard work, and watch all sorts of wildlife. I am driving a car or truck more often instead of taking a subway train or taxi. I am spending more time at home and listening to stories from people I grew up with, and laughing at some of the foolish things we all did when we were young. I enjoy seeing and talking with some of my old-time schoolmates and friends. Even though there's not many of us left, I enjoy them. When we do meet or talk, it's usually about current events or old past stories and tales we'd heard. Some of the stories are sad, and some are laughable. I do want to talk a little about some of those stories and events that stick with me even today. For example, on January 11, 2011, I got a call from someone telling me that Mr. James Russell had died. I was saddened to hear of his death. It was Mr. Russell who took me to the March on Washington in August of 1963.

Collard greens in my garden in Woodbridge, Virginia.

On February 19, 2011, there was a terrible fire not far from my house. The fire started around noon on the south side of Interstate 95 and spread to the northeast side of the highway close to Northern Virginia Community College and my house. I could see the burning fire was coming my way. I called 911 and was told to evacuate the premises. I took the outside water hose and sprayed my house and went inside to gather some important documents. Next, I drove my car over to Freedom High School's parking lot, which was right across the street from my house. I went back in the house and watched the fire as it kept coming closer and closer towards the college and me. I just kept praying that the fire would stay away. By now, there were many fire trucks on the site, and by 9:30 that night, the fire was under control. However, about 12:45 a.m. Sunday morning, the fire started again, and the fire trucks came back to the scene. That made it harder for me to sleep that night, which was now actually morning time. I didn't know if the fire was going to ignite a third time or not. But I did manage to go to church that Sunday morning. Guess what? Rain came that Sunday night.

A month after that terrible fire, I had another sleepless night. It was March 23, 2011, the night my favorite legendary movie star, Elizabeth Taylor, died. She was preceded in death by two other film actresses I admired: Jane Russell, who died in February of that same year, and Bette Davis, who died in October of 1989. When Ms. Taylor died, the first thing I thought of was the joy I got from working with her son Michael Wilding Jr. on the daytime soap opera *The Guiding Light*.

Sunday, April 10, 2011, I read in the *Washington Post* that film director Sidney Lumet died of lymphoma at his home in New York. I remember when I lived in New York and I was cast as an extra in his AMC-TV weekly series called *100 Centre Street*. Mr. Lumet looked at me and the other extras and told me that I looked like a judge, and he went on to cast me as one. He was a brilliant director. He only had to do a minimum of reshoots with me pretending to be a judge.

Sunday, February 12, 2012, was the night of the $54^{th}$ *Annual Grammy Awards* show. When I got home from church that day, I turned on the TV and saw the continuing news of Saturday night's death of Whitney Houston. The news film clip was showing a young Whitney in her teens singing in the chorus at her family's church, New Hope Baptist Church in Newark, New Jersey. As I was watching the film clip, I had a flashback of first seeing and hearing her sing back in the fall of 1983 at a club called Sweetwaters in New York. I had gone to the club mainly to see the headliner of the show, Cissy Houston, of whom I was a big fan and still am. The club was rather small but very chic and comfortable. Cissy came to the microphone and said, "I want to introduce you all to my daughter, Whitney." After that intro, Whitney, who couldn't have been no more than eighteen or nineteen, came to the microphone and sang "Somewhere Over the Rainbow." That young, tall, slim girl was phenomenal. ABSOLUTELY PHENOMENAL! With that angelic voice, I knew from that moment on that Whitney was heading for stardom. That same night at Sweetwaters, Cissy noticed that the guitarist, Cornell Dupree, was in the audience and she gave acknowledgment to him. He was one of the best guitar players in the music business. During intermission, I went over and told him how much I loved the way he made that guitar talk. He laughed and thanked me. I enjoyed that night at the club. Not only did I get to hear Cissy and Whitney sing, but I met Cornell Dupree. For anyone who's not familiar with Cornell Dupree's guitar playing, I suggest you listen to some of Aretha Franklin's early Atlantic Records recordings. As I continued to watch the Grammys that night of February 12, 2012, the producers listed a memorial on the big screen of various people who died that past year. To my surprise and heartfelt feeling, on that memorial list was the name Cornell Dupree. Most of the *54$^{th}$ Annual Grammy Awards* show really put me in a very depressed mood that night. Whitney and Dupree, both gone.

    The next day, Monday, February 13, 2012, I met with Dr. Sam Hill, Provost of Northern Virginia Community College. Dr. Hill explained to me about an upcoming construction project that would be taking place sometime that year near my property. He showed me the projected plans and stated that I may incur some disturbances. I replied by telling him that when Freedom High School was being constructed, I had a lot of dust disturbances. The school sits directly in front of my house, and during the construction of that high school, the dust nearly drove me crazy. That was very kind and professional of Dr. Hill to let me know what was happening next to my property.

    After we finished discussing the future construction project, I told Dr. Hill some of the history of Woodbridge. I let him know that before the college was built, there was a spring between the college and Interstate 95. I went on and told him how my family and other Coloreds used to get drinking water from that spring, and how we washed clothes right there at it. I let Dr. Hill know that my family used an old galvanized tub, Octagon soap, and a washboard in order to wash clothes. As I got ready to tell Dr. Hill more about this area, he asked me to hold on because he wanted his secretary to hear what else I had to say. When she came to his office, I continued telling some of the history of this area. I told them how my family used to pick wild berries on the side of the road and would make a meal from those berries. I even told them how difficult it was for me going to school. But I also let them know that, despite the Jim Crow laws of that time, most of the Blacks and Whites around here got along quite well. Some of the information mentioned in the chapter "My

Life Growing Up in Virginia" was also told to Dr. Hill and his secretary. Just as I was finishing up my story with them, we all had teared up. Thank God for the box of Kleenex on Dr. Hill's desk. He asked me would I speak to a leadership group. I told him I would. So, on April 11, 2012, I did speak to a leadership group at the college. Basically, I told the group the same things I had told Dr. Hill and what I've already written about here. The group was in awe after I told them about my growing up here in Virginia.

In January of 2015, one of my childhood friends named Elenora stopped by to say hello to me and to see how I was doing. We chatted over three hours on what it was like growing up here in Woodbridge. She told me how her husband Benny used to beat her. The house they lived in was very small, and the house was cold in the winter and hot in the summer. In front of their house was another house where Benny's aunt and grandmother lived. A third house, which was about 15 or 20 feet off to the side of both houses, was the house where Elenora's parents lived. Well, late one evening, Elenora and Benny were visiting Elenora's parents. Benny had been drinking and was running his mouth, as he usually did when he got drunk. He just kept on trying to provoke an argument with Elenora. He told Elenora's father he was going to beat her ass. Elenora's father said, "You better not do it here. Take her home." Benny just wouldn't shut up. He was drunk as a skunk. Finally, Elenora got tired of listening to Benny's threats and decided to go home. But before she went home she asked her father could she borrow a hammer. Her father asked her what she wanted a hammer for. She told him that she needed it to hang a picture. The father obliged and told her to make sure he gets his hammer back.

Elenora took the hammer, went home, and got herself prepared for what was about to happen that night. She was sick and tired of her husband beating her all the time. She put a chair up against the door of the house, which only had one door and two or three windows. She waited and waited. At last, she heard a banging on the door. Benny shouted, "Bitch, open that door. I'm gonna beat your damn ass. I said open that damn door, didn't I?" Elenora was scared to death, but she wouldn't open that door. On the outside of the house, Benny was mumbling, cursing, and acting crazy. Obviously, he was still very drunk. He went to the outside window of the house and lifted the window halfway up, just enough to get his leg partially inside. Why in the world did he do that! Once he got part of that leg through the window, Elenora, with the hammer in her hands, went to town banging and banging on that leg. Benny fell back on the ground and was cussing, screaming, and hollering. He was in terrible pain, but somehow he made it next door to his aunt's and grandmother's house. The next day, the grandmother told someone that Elenora didn't have to break her grandson's leg.

Elenora was not the only Colored woman that suffered at the hands of an abusive Colored man. There was Henrietta, who hadn't been home no more than four or five days from giving birth at a hospital when her husband pulled her out of their house, threw her on the ground, and started beating her. I went up to him and said, "Man, stop that! She just had a baby! Don't do that." He stopped, got in his car, and left. I helped Henrietta get off the ground and back inside her house. I asked her if she was all right, and she said she was okay. Then I went home. I really felt sorry for her because of the abuse she went through. A few years later, I saw that same man physically take a hubcap off the wheel of his car and with that hubcap beat his wife in the head.

Then there was Lula Ann, a Colored woman whose boyfriend used to throw her to the ground and walk all over her. According to Lula Ann, the boyfriend even tried to suffocate her by putting her head down between the cushion of a Jennifer Convertible sofa. When I think of what some Colored women went through here in Virginia, it brings to mind the documentary I saw on the life of Tina Turner and how her husband Ike Turner abused her.

Then there was the abuse my sister, Sis, got from the third man that had impregnated her. I remember one particular incident in which Sis ran from the inside of the house to the outside. Once outside, she would run, cry, and scream, "Leave me alone. Leave me alone. Please stop it. Please!" When she ran back inside the house, the abuser was still following her. I was mad as hell at that man for beating up on my sister. I jumped in his face and told him to leave my sister alone. He punched me in the face and knocked me completely out. When I became conscious, I was lying on the floor with my head next to the foot of an old RCA Victrola that was used for playing records known as 78s and 45s.

There was another time I remember quite well. It was the time I went to visit my aunt Alberta, who lived further over in Woodbridge right off Davis Ford Road. I would often go there, do yard work, and cut the grass for her. She always fixed lunch for me and we'd sit at the kitchen table and talk. She told me all sorts of stories about our family, and I enjoyed listening and being with her. But on one occasion, she told me something that made me feel very sad. She said that her husband beat her, especially whenever she returned home from having taken some food over to my sister, her kids, and me. Every time I got ready to leave Aunt Alberta's home, she'd tell me if I see her husband out in the yard as I'm leaving, please don't tell him what we talked about. Apparently, she felt if he knew what we had talked about, he would truly beat her again. She went on to say that her husband was a mean man.

One of Alberta's five sisters, Fannie Jo, was said to have shot and killed a man. She left Virginia and moved to Pennsylvania to live. Some say the reason for the killing was because the man had assaulted her. And that every year, Fannie Jo's mother, Ora Bell, would leave Virginia and travel to Pennsylvania, most likely to see Fannie Jo. What's so unfathomable to me is why some men were so brutal, cruel, and abusive to the women. I have trouble trying to figure out why the women just didn't leave, like Fannie Jo did. The more I think about it now, they probably were afraid to leave, not knowing what would happen to them if they did.

Years later, and having moved back to Virginia, I asked an elderly lady, who was approaching 100 years of living, "Why was that? Why didn't the abused women just pack up and leave? Why stay with an abusive man?" The elderly lady looked at me and said nonchalantly, "Son, it's just the way it was back then."

Despite everything I've gone through and witnessed, life is still good. I am still getting small acting roles. Oh! Let me correct that. "There's no such thing as small acting roles, only small actors." Recently, I was asked to act in an upcoming production of playwright August Wilson's play *Fences*, but because of other commitments, I declined. In the summer of 2022, I was cast as a UAW (United Auto Worker) in the Netflix film called *Rustin*. It is based on Bayard Rustin, who was very instrumental in the conceiving of the 1963 March on Washington. Yes, life is good.

Since moving back to Virginia, I've directed a few well-known plays. Among them are Lorraine Hansberry's *A Raisin in the Sun*, Emily Mann's *Having Our Say*, and James Baldwin's *The Amen Corner*.

Today, most of the people who live near what was once called "Kankey Hill" have no idea what it was. Only a few living Blacks are around to remember Kankey Hill, and I doubt if there are any Whites. The area is now more of a metropolis and an exclusive neighborhood. There are upscale stores, condos, townhouses, restaurants, car dealers, and is in close vicinity to public transportation. According to a study done in 2015, this area is now one of the best places to live in Northern Virginia. I'm proud to be near this place once known as Kankey Hill.

**THE END**

Made in the USA
Middletown, DE
13 November 2024

64540495R00077